# BEFORE THE GOLD RUSH

# BEFORE THE GOLD RUSH

*The Sinclairs of Rancho del Paso 1840-1849*

CHERYL ANNE STAPP

ISBN-13: 9781542983167
ISBN-10: 1542983169
Library of Congress Control Number: 2017902039
CreateSpace Independent Publishing Platform
North Charleston, South Carolina

*Dedicated to the amazing, pioneering men and women whose energies and sacrifices created civilization in the remote 1840s Sacramento Valley wilderness.*

# CONTENTS

# ACKNOWLEDGEMENTS

Accurate historical treatises are impossible without the input of many diverse and interested individuals who are experts in their field. The author wishes to gratefully thank the knowledgeable librarians at the California State Library, Sacramento; History and Educational Programs Lead Steve Beck at Sutter's Fort State Historic Park, and Nancy Jenner, Curator at Sutter's Fort SHP. Also, heartfelt thanks go to John R. Barlow, Curator for Business, History and Social Sciences at the New York Public Library, for providing a copy of New York's Official Probate Records containing John Sinclair's Last Will and Testament.

# ROSTER

**A partial roster of the Sinclair's friends and contemporaries...**

*Joseph Ballinger Chiles* (1810-1885). Venerable pioneer who came to California in 1841 with the Bartleson-Bidwell Party, the first group of organized American settlers to cross the Sierra Nevada. Between 1842 and 1853 Chiles crossed the continent another seven times, leading more wagon trains west. In 1844 he received the Rancho Catacula in Napa Valley as a Mexican land grant, and in 1850 he purchased part of the Rancho Laguna de Santos Calle in Yolo County.

*The Donner Party* (1846-47). A group of several families who separated from the main westward-bound wagon caravan of 1846 to follow a "shortcut" that cost them too much time, and subsequently became trapped at a small Sierra Nevada alpine lake in the stormy winter of 1846-47. Brimming with heroism and villainy, their story remains the most sensational and haunting in the annals of western migration.

*John Charles Frémont* (1813-1890). A United States Army officer and explorer, commissioned to describe and map the largely uncharted West. Court-martialed for his activities during the Mexican-American War, he was nonetheless a popular hero during his lifetime. His exploration reports, published by Congress, were widely read by an enthralled and adoring American public, and convinced thousands that the West was not only desirable, but attainable.

*Eliab Grimes* (1780-1848). Born in Massachusetts, by 1818 Grimes was a widely experienced mariner and trans-Pacific trader. The owner of several vessels engaged in the sea otter trade, he also acted as agent for John Jacob Astor and several other prominent shipping firms, in the Bering Strait and elsewhere. Eliab Grimes was among the first to establish commerce between Hawaii and California in the hide and tallow trade; and for twenty years owned a successful mercantile in Honolulu.

*Sarah Montgomery* (1825-1905). Sarah and her husband Allen came to California with the Stephens-Murphy-Townsend Party in 1844, the first immigrants to bring wagons over the Sierra. A reputed beauty, Sarah had poor judgment when it came to men. Allen deserted her shortly after the Mexican-American War and her next husband, popular Talbot Green, was exposed as a fugitive bank embezzler named Paul Geddes who scuttled home to Pennsylvania to "clear his name," never to return. Sarah at last found happiness when she married Santa Clara lawyer Joseph Wallis (later Judge Wallis) in 1854. During the 1870s Sarah Montgomery Wallis was an active member of the California suffragette movement.

*James & Margret Reed.* Starting west from their home in Illinois, the Reeds were at first prominent members of the Donner Party, until James was exiled from the company weeks before the rest were trapped in the Sierra snows. One of just two families that escaped the mountain ordeal intact, the Reeds settled in San Jose, where they prospered. Margret died there in 1861; James in 1874. Their daughter Martha (nicknamed Patty) is best remembered for the little doll she kept hidden in her pocket during the months of entrapment at the lake camp.

*Pierson B. Reading* (1816-1868). One of the more prominent and important men in the early history of California, New Jersey-born Pierson Reading arrived at

Sutter's Fort in November 1843 with Joseph Chiles's all-male party of desperate riders. In 1844 Reading became the grantee of the northernmost Mexican land grant ever awarded: 26,632 acres on the Sacramento River near the foot of Mt. Shasta. His spectacular gold discovery in Shasta and Trinity counties in the summer of 1848 proved the hitherto unrealized immensity of the gold fields. During 1848-1850 Reading owned a store in Sacramento, and was a candidate for California governor in 1851.

*Jared Sheldon* (1813-1851). A carpenter by trade, Sheldon was one of the earliest employees at Sutter's Fort. In January 1844 he received the Omochumney Rancho as a Mexican land grant, 22,000 acres stretching along the Cosumnes River. In 1847, he constructed the second grist mill in the entire Sacramento Valley. One of many tragic casualties of the California Gold Rush, Sheldon was killed on July 12, 1851 by angry gold miners, for building an irrigation dam on his own property that flooded their upstream claims.

*John Sutter* (1803-1880). A Swiss citizen, Sutter arrived in the Sacramento Valley in August 1839, intent on founding a colony in what was then a wilderness. Receiving a Mexican land grant he named New Helvetia, Sutter constructed a spacious, high-walled trading post known to all as Sutter's Fort, which quickly became a Mecca for skilled tradesmen who needed jobs, and trail-weary overlanders in covered wagons. In January 1848 gold was discovered at his nearly finished sawmill, sparking the great California Gold Rush; later that same year Sacramento city was surveyed and mapped on his personal real estate. When lawless gold-rushers wrecked havoc on his manufacturing and agricultural empire at Sutter's Fort, Sutter retreated to his second farm on the Feather River, leaving California for good in 1865 after an arsonist burned his home at Hock Farm to the ground.

*George Yount* (1794-1865). Born in North Carolina, George was ten when his family moved to Missouri. He never learned to read or write, but he became a skilled hunter and learned the rudiments of carpentry and shingle making. He married in 1818. Eight years later George sold his farm, gave the proceeds to his wife and children, and left them to seek his fortune as a fur trapper. His travels brought him to California, via Cajon Pass, in 1831. He hunted sea otter for a time, and was later hired to repair the mission buildings at Sonoma. Meanwhile, believing him dead, his wife remarried. In 1835 Yount became a naturalized Mexican citizen and in 1836, the grantee of the 12,000-acre Rancho Caymus in Napa Valley.

# INTRODUCTION

Many ghostlike figures languish in the shadows of California's past, duly acknowledged by name in various books and documents, yet lacking that fleshier substance which would allow them a more prominent treatment in the historical record. Among these "ghosts" are John and Mary Eyre Sinclair, who resided on a 44,000-acre Sacramento Valley ranch long before the land itself acquired national fame in the 1880s as a breeding farm for James Haggin's derby-winning thoroughbreds.

The ranch was two miles east of John Sutter's trading post. Before and during the California Gold Rush, Scots-born John Sinclair was an important man in the Sacramento District, characterized by Thomas Oliver Larkin, U.S. Consul to Mexican California, as a man of property and respectability who had influence on those around him.[1] Yet today he is presented as merely an interesting peripheral character in the several book-length biographies of John Augustus Sutter, most of which simply repeat two statements lifted from the pages of Hubert Bancroft's *History of California*: that Sinclair worked for the Hudson's Bay Company in Oregon for "some years," and that he edited a newspaper in Honolulu. Bancroft gives no source for these statements but quite likely took them almost verbatim from Captain William Dane Phelps' memoir *Fore and Aft* published in 1871.

As will be shown, John Sinclair resided in Oregon Territory for slightly less than a full year.

None of the Sutter biographies mention Mary Sinclair at all.

John Sinclair deliberately relocated to California as a direct result of meeting John Sutter in Hawaii. As for Mary, an act of kindness out on the wide prairies completely changed her life.

The Embarcadero (landing place) on the Sacramento River, four miles west of Rancho del Paso. Sketched in October 1848, the view is to the east toward the future location of I Street in the city of Sacramento. —Courtesy Sutter's Fort Museum Collections.

*Chapter 1*

MARY

Mary Eyre entered the United States at New Orleans on January 30, 1843, aboard the ship *England* from Liverpool. According to the passenger manifest she was fifteen and-a-half years old, traveling with her mother Eliza Turner Eyre and five other children: Thomas, aged thirteen; Eliza, ten and-a-half; Amelia, seven and-a-half; Mesina, thirteen and-a-half; and an infant named Henry. Mrs. Eyre's occupation was noted as a dressmaker, and the family's stated destination was St. Louis, Missouri, to join her husband Miles Eyre. Mrs. Eyre, who was thirty-seven, told authorities she was thirty-four, thus lowering her real age from getting-on-toward forty to nearer-thirty.[2] Now, however, Mrs. Eyre faced a far more serious situation than explaining away a harmless bit of female vanity. She was going to have to tell her husband of eighteen years the dreadful truth that at least one of the children accompanying her weren't his, but the result of another man's attention and affection after Miles left England to explore opportunities in America.

The date of Miles Eyre's arrival in America is uncertain. Vague family statements made many years later claim that he preceded them by about two years, departing England in early 1841, but it must have been earlier than that. The law required an alien to reside in the United States for two years before making application for citizenship, and Miles in fact applied for naturalization in St. Louis County, Missouri, on March 24, 1842. Allowing for an average sea voyage from Liverpool to New Orleans of about fifty-five days (although less than a full month under optimum conditions), plus travel time upriver to St. Louis and perhaps a few weeks to settle in there, he had to have left England no later than the latter half of 1839.

According to his middle daughter Eliza, Miles Eyre was "One of the pioneer settlers of the city of St. Louis, and one of the earliest merchants there." Her accolade reflects the displaced pride of family lore since St. Louis, incorporated as a city in 1823, already had a bustling, cosmopolitan population of 16,500 by 1840, teeming with merchants. He is listed in the 1842 St. Louis Directory as "Eyres, Miles, locksmith and manufacturer of saws & cutlery at 72 N. Second." [3] His status in the city's merchant hierarchy aside, Miles Eyre was a disagreeable, domineering, short-tempered man. One can imagine the firestorm that surely erupted when his family reached St. Louis, where he was confronted with the evidence of his wife's adultery. That, and her unforgiveable effrontery in daring to bring the baby, or babies, to America—for there may have been two love children instead of just one.

Indeed, Eliza's second husband James Campbell, in his divorce proceedings against her in August 1848 on the grounds that she was an abusive wife and unfit mother, coupled with his petition for custody of their daughter Susannah and their yet unborn son John, accused her thus: "During the absence of her former husband to the United States…she had children by another man…which children were left at St. Louis, Missouri."

Clearly, the infant Henry was sired by someone else. The puzzle is the girl Mesina. If, as recorded on the *England*'s passenger list she was thirteen-and-a-half, she was probably a servant. It was not at all uncommon in England for the working-class poor to "enter service" at an early age. However, if her listed age was meant to be stated in months, not years, and therefore born approximately November 1841, there was sufficient time after Miles's departure for Mesina to also have been Eliza's child with another man—note James Campbell's use of the plural *children*. Mesina and Henry were not with the Eyre family when they journeyed west later that year, and neither of these children was ever publicly mentioned again by any Eyre family member, although Susannah (later Mrs. Ira Woodin) and John Campbell were affectionately accepted by the four Eyre siblings.[4]

## Bound for Oregon

But whether it was one or two ill-born babes, Miles Eyre evidently intended to put distance between himself and the fruits of his wife's betrayal. Legally, women were non-persons, the property of their husbands and fathers. Miles could self-righteously ignore anything that his wife or maturing eldest daughter Mary might feel about abandoning two innocents who were unable to fend for themselves. Probably, this was when Miles began using his fists on both of them to vent his rage at being cuckolded.

In 1843 migration to Oregon was the talk of the Missouri frontier. Miles might already have selected this destination even before he was influenced and aided by physician Dr. Marcus Whitman, a Presbyterian missionary and enthusiastic promoter of American colonization in Oregon Territory, which was jointly owned by England and the United States. Dr. Whitman, on his celebrated and arduous ride eastward from his Waiilatpu mission near Fort Walla Walla in the winter of 1842-43, rested in St. Louis for two or three days in early March 1843, where he was a guest of Dr. Edward Hale. Almost immediately upon arrival, Whitman was besieged by a flood of visitors wanting to know both the particulars and the future possibilities for American settlers in the Oregon Territory. Could wagons really be taken all the way, as Whitman so often and so strongly asserted? According to historian Clifford Drury, Miles Eyre's shop was a meeting place for many who were thinking of going to Oregon, and a member of that group must have persuaded Dr. Whitman to come talk with them.[5] John Hobson, eighteen in 1843 and the son of Mrs. Miles Eyre's future third husband, wrote to Reverend Myron Eells many years later to describe his experiences as an emigrant to Oregon. Hobson's letter, dated January 30, 1883, at Astoria, Oregon, was published in Eells' book, *Marcus Whitman, M.D. Proofs of his Work in Saving Oregon.*

> *My father's family came to St. Louis in March 1843, from England, on our way to Wisconsin, but on account of snow and ice in the river we could not proceed, and while detained there we met the Doctor [Whitman] and several others, who were talking of coming to Oregon; so, by his description of the country, and proffered assistance in getting here free of charge, my father with family, and Miles Eyres and family, Messrs. Thomas Smith, a Mr. Ricord, and J. M. Shively, all agreed to come...The Doctor assisted Eyres and my father in purchasing wagons and mules in St. Louis. We went to Westport, through the state of Missouri, to the rendezvous, and the rest went by river. I do not know whether the Doctor was going to or on the return from Washington, but we did not see him any more until we met him at the Indian mission [the Shawnee Mission], a few miles from Westport, in the early part of May, where he assisted us in getting more teams and horses.*

Whitman continued on his eastward journey to Atlantic states cities where he met with a mission board committee, high-level United States government officials, and New York *Tribune* editor Horace Greeley. Following a family visit to Illinois, he was back in St. Louis by May 12 to accompany the emigration, although he remained at the Shawnee Mission, technically the Shawnee Indian Manual Labor School near Westport, until May 31, before joining the caravan. Meanwhile, wagon companies were independently organized by Weston, Missouri lawyer Peter Burnett, St. Clair County farmer Jesse Applegate, and many others. These companies began gathering along the Kansas River at Big Springs in early May to await the time when prairie grasses were high enough to provide animal forage, growth which came late in the 1843 season. The assembly was larger than in any previous year, consisting of 120-150 wagons, more than 900 individuals, and thousands of livestock. The first wagons, of what the press soon labeled "The Great Migration," began rolling westward from various camps on Monday, May 22. Their pilot was former Army officer-turned-fur trader Captain John Gantt, hired to lead them as far as Fort Hall in present-day Idaho. Delayed by their need for further assistance from Dr. Whitman in purchasing additional supplies and draft animals at Westport, the Eyre family left the frontier settlements with a group of other stragglers. They were a week behind the main body of emigrants, in a train organized and captained by Daniel Waldo, thus putting them at the rear of the larger caravan. The forward wagons reached the Kaw (Kansas) River on May 26, and by May 31 the majority of the travelers had all been safely ferried across on a crudely-built raft consisting of two dugout canoes supporting a single deck. This contraption must have instilled trepidation in the hearts of the womenfolk, and Mary Eyre when it was her party's turn to cross during the first week of June.[6]

Once across the Kaw the newly-formed Oregon Emigrating Company elected Peter Burnett as their captain, but dissention was already brewing. At issue was the estimated 3,000-5,000 head of loose cattle belonging to some of the more prosperous emigrants such as Jesse Applegate, versus those who had few or none. Those without resented having to stand guard at night over animals that didn't belong to them. Furthermore, they complained that the cattle were slowing them down, although right after the caravan crossed the West Fork of the Blue River, incessant thunderstorms created as much irritation as the livestock. Beset with quarrelsome followers without "excessive" herds who refused to proceed with those who did, Burnett resigned on June 8. He was replaced with William Martin; nevertheless, the company split. Emigrants having large herds of loose cattle set up their own train, naming Jesse Applegate as their captain. The Eyre family was not driving a large herd, but their leader Daniel Waldo was a friend and former neighbor of Jesse Applegate. The Eyres and the rest of Waldo's followers henceforth loosely attached themselves with Applegate's "Cow Column." [7]

Trailing several days behind the Oregon Emigrating Company was the forty-member exploring expedition of U.S. Army Lieutenant John Charles Frémont, and a much smaller group in mule-driven wagons led by Joseph Ballinger Chiles. Chiles, who was returning to California after his first journey there in 1841 with the Bidwell-Bartleson Party, was taking a calculated, though optimistic, chance that he could get his party into California with their wagons intact. In '41 the Bidwell Party had abandoned their wagons in the desert at the Utah-Nevada border. Somehow they missed the Truckee River leading to the shortest way into California, and straggled into the San Joaquin Valley somewhere north of the Sonora Pass on foot and horseback. They had not blazed a suitable wagon trail over the Sierra and therefore, since no other overlanders had gone to California in 1842, none yet existed. The company of 1841 had made their perilous trip with a woman and a toddler. This year Chiles was starting out with a few greenhorn men, three women, and five young children.

Accompanying Chiles were several individuals who were to play a significant part in altering young Mary Eyre's destiny. William "Billy" Baldridge, a successful dealer in milling machinery, was a close friend of Chiles. Teenaged Elizabeth Yount and her married sister Frances were the daughters of Chiles' former neighbor George Yount. They wanted to reunite with their father, who had settled in the Napa Valley years earlier. College-educated Julius Martin and his wife Elizabeth McPherson Martin were going to California because they had heard favorable reports of the soil and climate. Frances Yount Vines and her husband Bartlett had two young daughters. The Martins had three daughters under five: Mary, Arzelia, and infant Martha. Billy Baldridge, a thirty-one-year-old bachelor, was ambitiously taking along a full set of mill-irons, including three sash saws, for a mill he and Joe Chiles intended to build in California.[8] In early June, beyond the Kaw River, nineteen-year-old John Boardman—who was keeping a journal—and his male companions "fell in" with the Chiles Party, or, considering that no roster of the original group survives, possibly had been attached to it from the outset.

Chiles' company managed to overtake segments of the Oregon wagons, thereafter traveling with some of them, or slightly ahead of or behind others, as trail opportunities dictated. Just when Joseph Chiles and his party first began traveling in close proximity with the Miles Eyre family is unrecorded. Perhaps during mid-June, while the emigrants were wending their way along the rain-swollen Blue River, or not until July, when they reached the forks of the Platte River. In any event, intermittent rain showers kept river levels high and the emigrants' clothing soaked.

A number of wagons rolled into Fort Laramie on July 13 and 14, where several Indian tribes were camped outside the fort's white-washed adobe walls with horses, moccasins, and other goods to sell or trade. On the nights of July 14 and 15, the emigrants enjoyed lively dances at smaller Fort Platte a mile away, but we don't know if Miles, whose foul temper had become apparent to everyone around him, allowed Mary to attend the festivities. Mary's own recollection of that time is more interesting: at Fort Laramie an old Indian chief offered 100 horses for her—a pale-complexioned, flaxen-haired girl who had recently turned sixteen—and was surprised and chagrined when his offer was refused.[9] Mary does not say who else witnessed this exchange. But by then her family was in close daily contact with the Chiles Party, which had increased significantly near the forks of the Platte with the addition of several Oregon-bound single men who had, mid-journey, opted for California.

Leaving Fort Laramie July 16, the trail wound through the low, carved-up Black Hills, so named for the dense cedar that grew upon them. On a stretch of rough and broken trail they passed the heartrending grave of a six-year-old—the first fatality of the 1843 migration—whose playful antics had thrown him beneath the wheels of his father's wagon. Four days later, while Chiles and company were camped on Squaw Creek, they encountered the renowned mountain-man Joseph R. Walker, who was on his way to Fort Laramie to sell a substantial quantity of furs. Chiles, who had known Joe Walker in Missouri, was delighted to find him, and promptly engaged him to guide them to California for a fee of $300. The deal struck, Walker went on east to Fort Laramie to dispose of his furs, but soon returned to lead the company to Fort Bridger on Black's Fork of the Green River. They arrived on August 13 to find fur-trapper Jim Bridger's new trading post half-destroyed and deserted, as the result of an earlier vandalism by Cheyenne Indians. Bridger and his partner Louis Vasquez were absent, having left to visit other trapper friends before the raid occurred. Nevertheless, the locale offered good pasture and water. Joe Walker set his charges to hunting and drying meat for the journey ahead, activities that lasted nearly two weeks, but didn't go as well as Walker hoped. The raiding Cheyenne had also scattered the game, plus the outfit lost a considerable portion of their dried meat by carelessly leaving it where their dogs found and devoured it.[10]

## An Intervention

At this campground—as at previous sites—the travelers were subjected to the frequent angry screaming and anguished wails emanating from the Eyre wagon as Miles Eyre cruelly beat his wife and oldest daughter with his fists and a stinging lash. Everyone had tried to ignore these outbursts, and Eyre's frequent verbal abuse of both women. Still, this incident was such a violent one that Joseph Chiles' friend Billy Baldridge, who saw Mary Eyre as a sweet-faced, innocent girl, could no longer stand the idea that she was being subjected to such brutal treatment. Resolving to liberate her from what he considered abject bondage, Baldridge first asked Mrs. Julius Martin if she would let Mary travel with her family to California if he could induce the girl to come with them. Elizabeth Martin, a capable and compassionate woman who was doubtless horrified by Mary's situation, readily agreed. Next he consulted with Mary's mother Eliza Eyre, who was only too glad to give her daughter a chance to escape. Last, Billy put the proposition to Mary, who immediately assented.

On Sunday, August 27, Miles went to the nearby Indian village in search of a horse that had wandered away, and while he was gone Eliza helped Mary pack her belongings. The following morning, August 28, Eliza smuggled Mary and the bags into the Martin's wagon just as the companies were pulling out. A torrent of abuse erupted when Miles discovered the subterfuge. Nonetheless, he managed to quickly separate the remaining family and their wagon from the campsite, whipping up his mules to catch up with another group headed for Oregon.

A month later, on September 26, Miles Eyre drowned in the Snake River at dangerous Three Island Crossing—in sight of his terrified family—a victim of his own obstinacy. Ignoring the advice of his fellow emigrants, he had insisted on driving his team into the river by himself. The frightened mules became unmanageable, turning upstream, and throwing Miles from his seat. He soon disappeared beneath the surging water. His body was never recovered and since all his money was strapped around his waist, his death left Mary's mother and younger siblings destitute. Dr. Marcus Whitman, who felt responsible for having encouraged Eyre to go in the first place, took Eliza and the children to his mission at Waiilatpu where they spent the winter of 1843-44.

Mary may not have learned of her father's death or the resulting circumstances of her family until she reached California many months later. Billy Baldridge began calling Mary his "Prairie Flower," but his intentions toward her were honorable and he remained her self-appointed guardian throughout and beyond the long, difficult journey.[11]

Meanwhile, on the day of Mary's rescue, the Chiles Party started toward Fort Hall, a Hudson's Bay Company outpost for the past six years, which had originally been established in 1834 by independent trapper Nathaniel Wyeth. The weather remained cold and cloudy, with intermittent rain showers. Hunters bagged two bears, and others caught fish, which were consumed before they reached Fort Hall fifteen days later on

Tuesday, September 12. There they learned that post commander Richard Grant, already overwhelmed by the needs of the forefront Oregon wagons, said he needed the fort's remaining supplies for his own employees and refused to sell meat, rice or flour at any price. Joseph Walker refused to take the group any farther unless their critical food shortage could be remedied. Joe Chiles finally managed to buy four beef cattle and other scant provisions at high prices, but Walker deemed these insufficient for what he estimated could be another sixty days of travel.

They decided to split the company, allocating the four cattle and the bulk of the food supplies to the wagons. Chiles would take a group of men on the best riding stock farther west to Fort Boise for provisions for themselves—and if this proved unsuccessful, they would live on the land until they reached Sutter's Fort in the Sacramento Valley. There, they planned to purchase supplies and bring them back east across the Sierra to the others via a route as yet undiscovered, while Walker led the rest: about twenty-five individuals, including the four women and five children. A third contingency allowed for the riders to bring relief provisions south from Sutter's Fort down California's great valley, because Walker expected to enter through a pass that flanked the southern end of the lofty Sierra Nevada. The entire company camped together a few miles west of Fort Hall for the last time on September 16, but not before Julius Martin—adamant that his wife and daughters would not go hungry—rode back with a companion to Fort Hall where both used "unpleasant means" to coerce a little more food from Richard Grant.

At this point John Boardman, miffed at not being invited to join the horseback riders, decided to continue on to Oregon. "Chiles appears to prefer having those go through with him to California, who have not traveled with him, than to have Smith and myself, thinking we could go with the wagons so that we would pay some of the pilotage" (a share of Walker's fee). Such are the words of complaint Boardman entered in his journal about Joe Chiles, and the few single men who had left the Oregon emigration at Fort Hall to join the California-bound party.[12] Boardman's departure is history's loss insofar as documenting the next part of Mary's journey to California, because none of those who followed Joseph Walker kept a trail diary. What little we know of it has been pieced together from various, and sometimes conflicting, statements the participants made in memoirs penned many years after the events.

## On to California

Sunday morning, September 17, each faction went its own way. Chiles took William Winter, John Wooden, Milton McGee, and Thomas Westly Bradley. Also the four Williams brothers James, John, Squire and Isaac; and the new recruits Pierson B. Reading, Captain John Gantt, Samuel J. Hensley, and possibly William Martin, the Oregon-train captain who had replaced Peter Burnett.[13]

Joseph Walker led the wagon company up the Raft River, through the spectacular City of Rocks and across the Goose Creek divide, to the Humboldt River and down its 360-odd mile length, a trip made even longer by the river's countless meanderings through canyons and plains, to the Humboldt Sink. There, the company halted on or about October 22 to await the arrival of the horseback party with fresh provisions. Unbeknownst to them, though, the riders had experienced their own hardships traveling southwestward along the Malheur River—entering California at its northeastern corner—and were still three weeks away from reaching Sutter's Fort. The season was growing late. Walker waited a few days and then pushed on, ordering a cut in daily rations.

We don't know what Mary thought of Joseph Walker but she must have been awed. In 1843 Walker was forty-five years old, a gigantic man six-feet-four inches tall and weighing more than 200 pounds. He was a widely-known, long-experienced trapper-explorer-mountain man who was always respectfully addressed as "Captain" though he had no military rank. Here was a man who effortlessly controlled his subordinates with soft-spoken directives instead of her father's contemptuous sneers, fists and lashes. Walker, who had explored much of the uncharted West including California, was a man whose very presence and demeanor calmed the fears of the wagon company members. Elizabeth and Julius Martin treated Mary kindly and she enjoyed the continuing protection of Billy Baldridge, who almost certainly discouraged attentions from the group's single men toward his Prairie Flower. And she was forming a close friendship with pretty Elizabeth Yount, who was only seven months older and unmarried.

From the Humboldt Sink Captain Walker led them south over mostly barren deserts. Beyond Carson Lake the company had a scare when Milton Little, on night guard duty, got an arrow in his chest from a Paiute lurking about their camp. Someone managed to remove the shaft but the arrow remained imbedded in his chest muscles, causing him great pain. No further attacks followed and at the next big lake (officially named Walker Lake a few years later), they were aided by friendlier Indians who traded fresh fish to them in exchange for horseshoe nails. But by the time they reached Owens Lake some 190 miles beyond, the mules were too exhausted to pull any farther, and the company was forced to abandon the wagons along with most of their household goods. Billy Baldridge suffered the greatest loss. He had to bury his mill irons, which he had hauled all the way from Missouri, in the hot sands. Packing a few personal belongings on the mules remaining after killing one for sustenance, the party, all mounted on horses, went on their way.[14] Most likely, the five young children were carried in panniers slung over the horses' backs, or rode in adult laps.

At eleven o'clock in the morning of December 3, 1843, the weary emigrants came to the summit of the pass Captain Walker had discovered on his departure from California back in 1834, crossing it without undue hardship through six inches of snow. As soon as they descended, several individuals were determined to immediately head north to Sutter's Fort. Walker restrained them at Four Creeks (modern-day Visalia), insisting on crossing the drought-ravaged central San

Joaquin Valley to the coast range, where he knew there would be abundant water and game. With some grumbling, they consented. On the week-long trek across the parched plains they endured three days without food or water, until they crossed over a grassy range and entered what was later named Peachtree Valley. It was a well-watered region teeming with wildlife. The company spent a few days resting and feasting on haunches of roast venison and the fat, palatable meat of wild horses. From there they followed San Lorenzo Creek to the Salinas River, moving up to the ruins of neglected Mission Soledad where they disbanded,[15] and hereafter the chronology, as recorded in various memoirs and documents, becomes vague. Captain Walker recruited Lewis Anderson, Fleurnaye Dawson, and Thomas Cowie to aid him in gathering a herd of horses and mules to drive to Santa Fe. This group departed for places unknown, resurfacing again at Monterey in February. While still near the Mission Soledad, William Baldridge and James "Old Wheat" Atkinson decided to ride into Monterey for passports. After being detained there for three days due to what Baldridge termed "indolence and indifference of the Mexican officials," the pair returned to the last campsite to find that the Martins and Vines had already gone on toward Sutter's Fort.[16]

Mary Eyre was still traveling with the Martin family, and Frances Yount Vines and her sister Elizabeth were likely eager to reach their father's Rancho Caymus in the Napa Valley. The Martins and Vines, and perhaps the few single men still with the company, journeyed on together until—as Julius Martin recollected—at the end of December they reached John Gilroy's ranchlands. Right then and there, Julius and Elizabeth Martin decided to stop and settle in the small village of San Ysidro (Old Gilroy).[17] Here, according to Billy Baldridge's second-hand reckoning, Elizabeth Yount convinced Mary to come live with Elizabeth's family in Napa instead of remaining with the Martins. Mary's parting from Julius and Elizabeth and their children was probably tearful but under the circumstances could not have been prolonged. Bartlett and

Frances Vines had their own two little daughters to consider, and needed to push on.

There is no record of Mary's and the Vines family's journey into the Sacramento Valley, but Billy's account of his own trek offers an example of travel from the coastal regions to the interior, and might have had similar aspects. Coming inland to the vicinity of modern Gilroy, Baldridge and Atkinson encountered two recent immigrants who provided them with fresh horses and escorted them to the Pueblo de San Jose, where merchant Charles Weber (the future founder of Stockton) took them on to Robert Livermore's ranch. From there they travelled diagonally across the San Joaquin Valley, crossed the San Joaquin River near the present site of Stockton and rode on to Sutter's Fort, probably arriving around the third week of January but possibly sooner; Baldridge did not specify his date of arrival. At Sutter's they were reunited with many of their former overland companions, members of the horseback party who had reached the fort on November 10 or 11, much too late to breach the snow-crusted high Sierra west-to-east. Even had this been possible, by then the Walker-guided wagon train was already ten days south of the Humboldt Sink anyway. Pierson Reading, Samuel Hensley, John Gantt and the Williams brothers had accepted employment with John Sutter. Joseph Chiles had already returned to the fort from a long pack train expedition south through the San Joaquin Valley, after unsuccessfully trying to locate Walker's party.[18] The Vines family, Elizabeth Yount, and Billy's Prairie Flower were already there, too.

And so was John Sinclair—a highly intelligent, likable and articulate Scot given to inventive verbal humor—who was Captain Sutter's sometime business associate and closest neighbor, northeast of him by about two miles. In January 1844 Mary Eyre was two months shy of turning seventeen. Sinclair was nearly eighteen years her senior, yet the attraction between them must have bloomed quickly—at least on his part—since, as Baldridge expressed it, John "forthwith laid siege to her hand and heart." Still committed to safeguarding Mary's well-being, Billy Baldridge "made inquiries" into the character and background of her ardent suitor.

## Chapter 2

# JOHN

For the past two years John Sinclair had been part-owner and resi-dent manager of the Rancho del Paso, a 44,000-acre spread across the American River from Sutter's Fort. Like all of the ranchers in 1840s California, he used Indian labor in his fields and as household servants. How many Indians John employed on a regular basis is unknown. As was customary, he paid them with goods such as shirts, blankets, and other small manufactured items obtained from the trading vessels that called at towns along the coast.

Sinclair's 1841 visitor, Captain William Dane Phelps, described John as "an intelligent Scotchman of considerable education, hardy and en-terprising." In his memoir *Fore and Aft*, Phelps recalled that "in connec-tion with his neighbor Captain Sutter, he managed to control a number of Indian tribes, among whom they found abundant help in cultivating their wheat fields and managing cattle." Also, from time to time, Sinclair employed Sutter's hangers-on at the fort in various capacities. Partnered with Eliab Grimes, a wealthy Honolulu sea captain and merchant who of-ficially owned the property, Sinclair was prospering from the sale of hides and tallow, the mainstay of the California economy.

While living in Hawaii he had married a native woman, now de-ceased, and proudly boasted that his five-year-old daughter was proficient in multiple languages even at that tender age. No doubt John shared this personal information with Billy Baldridge to dispel any notions which his earlier past suggested: that he was a vagabond adventurer unable or unwilling to assume the proper responsibilities of a caring husband to a parentally mistreated young woman.[19] For in Billy's view, Sinclair's past would certainly sound impetuous and adventure-filled, starting with John's participation in Nathaniel Wyeth's ill-fated expedition from New England to Oregon in 1832.

## Across the Continent

Nathaniel Jarvis Wyeth was a successful Cambridge, Massachusetts, ice merchant who determined to enter the then-lucrative fur trade in the Far West, and, further, to establish profitable salmon fisheries in the largely unknown Oregon country. He knew he had every right to do this. True, the fur trade in the vast Oregon Territory was dominated by the Hudson's Bay Company, a British firm—but the fact was, England and the United States had agreed to hold joint ownership of the region.

Wyeth's impetus sprang from his association with fellow townsman Hall Jackson Kelley's long-held and widely proselytized utopian ideals to colonize the Oregon Territory with American settlers. Hall, his mind aflame with sea captains' tales, and the published reports of the Lewis and Clark Expedition, believed that a large American colony would diminish England's claim of complete sovereignty in the Pacific Northwest. Most rational New Englanders thought Kelley was eccentric at best; half-crazy, at worst. Nonetheless, Nathaniel Wyeth, an educated, level-headed businessman, was an enthusiastic member of Kelley's American Society for Encouraging the Settlement of Oregon from its inception in 1829.

Two years later, disenchanted with Kelley's oft-postponed departure times, Wyeth decided to act on his own. He acquired investors and organized a joint-stock company composed of men who were willing to contractually commit for five years. Those men were to accompany him overland, and share in his expected profits from fur trapping and exported salmon. Twenty-four would-be explorers signed up and congregated in Baltimore, but three had second thoughts before the group even reached Liberty, Missouri.[20]

John Sinclair was residing in New York City on March 10, 1832, when Wyeth sent a note instructing him to meet the brig *Ida* at Baltimore later that month. Quite likely, John had been in New York for some while before 1832. This supposition is based on probate documents concerning his last will and testament, filed many years later. John's will named four siblings who still resided in New York, suggesting the possibility that John emigrated from Scotland with his parents, not as an independent adult.

Was Sinclair an affiliate member of Hall Kelley's Society? We don't know. Nathaniel Wyeth mainly found his recruits through word-of-mouth, and limited advertising. Perhaps, like fellow-recruit John Ball, Sinclair was dissatisfied with the livelihood he was engaged in and viewed Wyeth's audacious plan to conquer three thousand miles of largely uncharted territory as an irresistible high adventure. Sinclair was able to pay the requisite $40.00 contribution to Wyeth's joint stock company—a significant amount in 1832—plus purchase his personal equipment (mess kit, ammunition, knives, and so forth), and pay his transport from New York to Baltimore, an indication that he was employed in some skilled or professional capacity, or had generous family funds at his disposal.

Wyeth's already reduced party—none of whom had any frontiering or mountaineering experience—left Independence, Missouri, on May 12, 1832, for their grand expedition to Oregon. Luckily, experienced mountaineer William Sublette allowed them to join his larger brigade of trappers headed for the 1832 rendezvous at Pierre's Hole, Idaho, else all might have perished. Besides enduring hunger, exhaustion, the usual greenhorn fevers and intestinal ailments, Wyeth's men lost valuable equipment and experienced a dramatic, and traumatic, battle with hostile Indians a few miles south of Pierre's Hole. Wyeth's company, now further reduced to eleven loyal followers by desertions and one death en route, arrived at the Hudson's Bay Company's massive Columbia River headquarters post, Fort Vancouver, on October 29. Twelve days and another death later, Nathaniel

Wyeth received news that the ship he had sent around Cape Horn with supplies for his salmon venture had been wrecked at sea. Consequently eight of his men, including John Ball and John Sinclair, asked to be released from their contract. "I could not refuse," Wyeth recorded. "They had already suffered much and our number was so small... they were good men and persevered as long as perseverance would do good." [21]

## On to Hawaii

Five of the eight intended to return home immediately, but there were no ships calling at Pacific Northwest ports. Dartmouth College graduate John Ball taught school at Fort Vancouver over the winter months. Sinclair took some type of short-term employment with the Hudson's Bay Company, reportedly clerical in nature. In the spring, John Ball and John Sinclair acquired tools and seeds from the fort's chief factor John McLoughlin, built a crude cabin in the fertile Willamette Valley in the vicinity of modern Salem where a few retired Hudson's Bay Company trappers had settled, and commenced farming. The farming venture was successful, but both of them suffered from recurring attacks of malaria and fever, as well as the lack of the more sophisticated eastern society to which they were accustomed. Somewhat regretfully, they left the farm September 20, 1833, sold their produce at Fort Vancouver, and boarded the Hudson's Bay Company brig *Dryad* bound for the Sandwich Islands (Hawaii).[22] On November 4 the *Dryad* entered the bay of San Francisco at the same time as an American whaler: the *Helvetius* commanded by Captain George Brewster of New London, Connecticut.

Apparently, the whaling vessel presented an unexpected opportunity for another adventurous experience. Sinclair could simply have gone on to Hawaii in a sedate merchant brig to connect with another ship bound for other foreign ports, and eventually home, as did John Ball. Instead John Sinclair boarded the *Helvetius*, which left port November 27, 1833, and the crew continued their whaling activities for several more months. Loaded with more than 1,400 barrels of whale oil, the ship made for Hawaii where roiling ocean swells prevented its attempt to anchor at Lahaina, a chief commercial port. The *Helvetius* then turned toward Oahu, where fierce storms drove the ship onto the reef off Diamond Head on November 30, 1834. No one was hurt but within days the raging sea had smashed the rig farther down on the rocks, where it was at last abandoned after most of the cargo had been salvaged.[23]

That disaster, following so close on the heels of Nathaniel Wyeth's failed expedition, Sinclair's own illness-plagued months spent farming in Oregon, and his recent action-packed days aboard a whaling ship, must have convinced him to explore opportunities in the comparatively stress-free, balmy Islands. That same year, 1834, the Hudson's Bay Company opened a post in Honolulu under the direction of George Pelly, who thereafter routinely traded with his counterparts in Oregon and elsewhere. Sinclair, with his connection to Fort Vancouver's John McLoughlin, may have taken employment with Pelly for a time. In this capacity he might well have sailed back to Oregon one or more times, although his precise whereabouts and activities are unknown until the latter half of 1838.[24]

But did he ever edit an Island newspaper? Two men, an American sea captain and a Swedish scientist—who met Sinclair on separate occasions—said so in their own memoirs, without divulging even the smallest particular. Given the insular religious zeal then prevalent among Hawaii's Protestant missionary community in the 1830s, it seems unlikely that an outsider would have been allowed to edit one of their publications. Much more in tune with the sentiments of Island foreign residents was the English-language *Sandwich Island Gazette,* founded in 1836 and edited by Stephen Macintosh, an American who frequently socialized with Honolulu's small foreign merchant community. In August 1838, Macintosh took a two-week vacation to revive his flagging health. Possibly he arranged for John Sinclair—by then a merchant partnered with Boston-born Captain Eliab Grimes and his much younger nephew Hiram Grimes—to cover for him during that period.[25] It is also possible that John published a short-lived newspaper on his own, although this raises the question of where he obtained a printing press. In the end, the only proof we have of John's Hawaiian journalistic endeavors are the statements of two men who met him in California.

We don't know just when Sinclair became a partner with Eliab and Hiram Grimes, or the circumstances that led to this agreement. John and Hiram worked behind the counter at their shop at Nuuanu and Merchant Streets in Honolulu, which dealt in furs, blankets, sheep shears, American textiles and ready-made clothing; pearl buttons, horn combs, China silks, rice from Manila, and other sundry merchandise.

We do know the window of time in which Sinclair first met John Sutter. With California as his ultimate goal, Sutter had traveled overland from Missouri with a group of Oregon-bound missionaries, arriving at Fort Vancouver too late in the season to travel south through mountain passes. Accepting advice from Hudson's Bay Company officials, he sailed west from Oregon on one of their ships, planning to board another vessel in Hawaii that was outbound for California. He landed at Honolulu December 9, 1838, only to find that there was no California-bound ship in the harbor, and none expected anytime soon. During his five-month sojourn in the Islands Sutter made the acquaintance of every merchant and official in town, impressing all (and dazzling some) with his plans to create a colony in the Mexican-owned province where, he claimed, opportunities abounded for men who were willing to take risks. Eliab Grimes, among the first to open trade between Hawaii and California in the 1820s, was intrigued but made no commitments beyond selling a few articles on credit. Sutter departed Honolulu on April 29, 1839, aboard the brig *Clementine*, scheduled to call at Sitka, Alaska, before sailing down the coast to California.[26]

## California

John Sinclair was not too far behind, landing at Monterey in December 1839 after a month-long voyage. Sinclair's reasons for leaving what must have been a secure life in Hawaii can only be guessed at. Sutter's tantalizing talk could have led him to seek new adventure and fresh opportunity, or he came representing his partners to report on Sutter's viability as a potential trading partner. Probably, a little of both. Many years later Sutter told historian Hubert Bancroft that "John Sinclair...had been sent to California by Eliab Grimes, a rich merchant in the Sandwich Islands." Sinclair arrived at Sutter's fledgling trading post in the Sacramento Valley in early 1840, when the only signs of a permanent settlement were a few Hawaiian-style huts and a three-room, thatched-roof adobe structure, all erected by the contracted laborers Sutter had brought from the Islands and some Indians who lived in nearby villages. Sutter had not yet planted foodstuffs, but he was eager to enter the local fur trapping trade, a business for which he had gained some knowledge but had no practical experience.[27]

In his later life Sutter never mentioned what agreements or arrangements he made with John Sinclair during that early period, instead lumping Sinclair among the also unnamed "several white men" in his employ. Yet in June 1840, Sutter wrote to a California creditor, "I am waiting for answers from several places...Mr. Sinclair and me are waiting by the very first opportunity for funds from Oahu." That same year he wrote to rancher Antonio Suñol in San Jose explaining that he didn't have cash for goods purchased on credit, but "through the efforts of Mr. Sinclair, I will pay you in castor [beaver] furs." [28] Sinclair's presence—and his personal connections with Honolulu's prominent merchants—must have been welcome so soon after John Sutter's own arrival, and before Sutter's hunter-trapper friends Niklaus Allgeier and Sebastian Keyser arrived in August 1840. Sinclair had, after all, hunted and trapped with the Wyeth expedition and had successfully farmed in Oregon, albeit a different climate. Sutter had Hawaiian workers, but had had little time to learn their language. After five years in the Islands, Sinclair was very likely fluent in Hawaiian. Moreover, Sinclair was a well-educated man who could discuss Shakespeare and other luminary men of letters at the end of the work day, a boon companion to book-loving Sutter.

But whether at work or rest, fleas and mosquitoes plagued everyone in the little wilderness colony. The discomfort provoked John to complain in writing to teenaged William Heath Davis, then residing in Yerba Buena, whom John had known in the Islands as the stepson of the U. S. Consular Agent to the Kingdom of Hawaii. "I should like to have your company up here a week or two," Sinclair joked to young Davis, "that you might know the pleasure of letter writing in the midst of myriads of mosquitoes, while every line you wrote, you would be obliged to lay down your pen and enjoy the luxury of scratching for awhile." Nonetheless, he had decided to stay in California. After the obligatory one year residence in the Mexican province, Sinclair became a naturalized Mexican citizen in 1841.[29]

Over the next few months Sutter's settlement began to take shape, but the amount of tools, livestock, equipment, finished goods and supplies required to keep it afloat was enormous. By mid-year 1841, Sutter was deeply in debt to Hawaiian merchants as well as California ranchers, some of whom were growing quite irate. He dispatched Sinclair to Hawaii to make arrangements to settle some accounts and purchase more goods, with promises to pay later in beaver pelts. John sailed from San Francisco Bay aboard the *Lama* on August 9, 1841. He returned in November, sailing into Monterey on the *Julia Ann*, with an agreement that benefited Sutter, the Grimeses, and himself. The house of Grimes agreed to assume Sutter's Hawaiian (and certain other) debts, and in exchange would be repaid by Sutter with land in the Sacramento Valley. For the time being, Eliab and Hiram continued to reside in the Islands. John Sinclair had established a small farm on a portion of this land, and was already living on the property, when he took formal possession of the Rancho del Paso in early 1842. However, the official conveyance from Sutter to Eliab Grimes, Hiram Grimes, and John Sinclair was dated August 10, 1843. Although the Rancho del Paso was outside the boundaries of Sutter's New Helvetia land grant, Governor Alvarado had bestowed upon Sutter broad powers as a representative of the Mexican government on the northern California frontier, and the government raised no objections to this transfer. Wanting a more secure title, Eliab Grimes, as a naturalized Mexican citizen, formally petitioned for, and was awarded, the same grant on December 20, 1844, by Governor Manuel Micheltorena.[30]

Meanwhile, during 1841-1843 John Sinclair played host to some visitors who had come to inspect Captain John Sutter's New Helvetia outpost: sea captain William Dane Phelps from Boston, John Yates, an English sailor, and Dr. G. M. Waseurtz af Sandels, a Swedish scientist and naturalist.

Captain Phelps arrived first. He was master of the 398-ton *Alert*, a trading vessel. Since June 1840, Phelps had sailed from port to port along the California coast, selling goods brought from New England, and collecting hides and tallow from local ranchers. Some months earlier he had met John Sutter at the port in San Francisco Bay, and had invited him to dinner aboard the ship. Sutter, in turn, issued an open invitation to visit his budding settlement in the Sacramento Valley. In July 1841, Phelps was finally able to take a short vacation. Sailing up the Sacramento River in the *Alert's* pinnace with a few of its crew, he arrived at Sutter's embarcadero on Thursday, July 29, 1841. Though he was as tormented by fleas as everyone else, Phelps was impressed with the progress of Sutter's improvements. On Friday, John Sinclair joined the two of them for breakfast, after which Phelps rode over to visit Sinclair's ranch.

> *Our route lay over a beautiful plain, the soil apparently of a rich black mould, and affording abundant feed for cattle. Mr. Sinclair, who is a very intelligent and respectable man, has his establishment which consists of two neat white cottages, and huts for his Indians, on the right bank of the river, with large oaks in front. The margin of the American River on each side is shadowed by trees of large growth, the land is high and never overgrown, the soil is of the richest kind, and in fact the country hereabouts is delightful. Deer and antelope are abundant… the wheat crop having failed this year, he has been obliged to depend upon the hunt to support himself and from 20 to 30 Indians whom he has kept employed. In front of his house and at not more than a stone's throw from his door he can obtain any quantity of the richest salmon.* [31]

Captain Phelps' description suggests that Sinclair's small houses were whitewashed. Possibly, one of them was intended as lodging for Eliab

Grimes when he came to the Rancho del Paso for extended stays. The highlight of Phelps' visit was a two-day elk-hunting excursion as far up as the Feather River, with John Sinclair and one of Sutter's trappers. He does not say more about John's two cottages, but does tell us that he and Sinclair formed a closer friendship when the two departed in Phelps's boat on August 3 to sail downriver. The trip to San Francisco Bay took five days; Phelps rejoined the *Alert* on August 8. As noted previously, Sinclair boarded the *Lama* for Hawaii to transact business for John Sutter. Captain Phelps returned to the Sacramento Valley on April 2, 1842. He and John took a fifteen-mile ride through the countryside on Monday, April 4, and again Phelps' journal expresses his pleasure in the landscape of the Rancho del Paso, saying, "Nothing can exceed the beauty and richness of the lovely plains covered with luxuriant feed and a vast quantity of flowers of every hue...The woodlands consist of oak and maple trees of large growth, and so clear of underwood and brush as to resemble an English park." The two enjoyed a game hunt the following day, but this time the visit was shorter. Captain Phelps left on Wednesday to return to his ship. [32]

John Yates, an inveterate wanderer since his adolescent days in Liverpool, stepped ashore at Yerba Buena sometime in the spring/summer of 1842. There he met Captain Sutter, who promptly hired him to captain the schooner *Sacramento,* acquired from the Russians as part of Sutter's purchase of Fort Ross. Before settling into his new duties, though, Yates—a man whose addiction to hard liquor caused him to later wreck Sutter's prized watercraft—took a horseback tour of the countryside, meeting John Sinclair shortly after riding out from Sutter's establishment. Yates' brief description contains a classic confession of his own favorite pastimes:

> *I came to Captain Grimes' Ranch on the American River. The house was constructed of mud and roofed with tula* [tule] *after the manner of all the first dwellings of settlers in this section of country. Grimes* [had gone to the Sandwich Islands] *and a Mr. Sinclair was left in charge of affairs at*

*the ranch. I found the latter a talented man and capital company where grog and cards were stirring.*[33]

A far more distinguished and reputable personage arrived in Alta California by sea at the end of September, 1842. Dr. Sandels, who was enjoying a world tour, made the rounds of the coastal communities. In the summer of 1843, he found Sutter's schooner anchored on the coast and boarded it for a trip upriver. "As I was an old friend of Captain Eliab Grimes," he recounted, "I took with me some agricultural implements for his partner, Mr. Sinclair." Upon landing at Sutter's embarcadero on the Sacramento River, Dr. Sandels was greeted warmly and treated to Sutter's generous hospitality. A while later, Sinclair arrived at the still-under-construction fort to welcome the visitor and receive his cargo from Eliab Grimes. Sandels described Sinclair as "a native of Scotland, a most intelligent and industrious man, whose conversation was very lively and interesting. For some years he had led a hunter's life in the Rocky Mountains, being under engagement as clerk in the Hudson's Bay Company."

The following day Sandels visited the Rancho del Paso—also still under development—where Sinclair served him a breakfast of tea cakes, and beef roasted on a ramrod (a metal bar, or rod, used for ramming the charge down into the barrel of a muzzle-loading firearm). While he didn't paint any word pictures of Sinclair's abode, the observant scientist did appreciate the fresh air wafting from the river where the house was situated. Of particular interest is his statement that Sinclair had Sandwich Islanders as servants, "though being himself most adept in his pursuits, he needed less aid in taking care of cattle than the majority of foreigners here." The implication is that the Islanders were domestic help rather than *vaqueros,* but that doesn't tell us how many Hawaiians worked for Sinclair, or when and how he acquired their services. They might have been members of the Hawaiian crew that arrived with Sutter in 1839, or new employees Sinclair had brought back with him from his 1841 trip to the Islands.

Sinclair and his guest rode about a landscape wooded with oaks, sycamores, willows, a few ash trees, lindens and cottonwoods where John—noted by Sandels as an excellent marksman—felled an antelope with a single shot. The deer, John explained, had been scared from the neighborhood by the white men and so hunting had become "very fatiguing." Dr. Sandels recorded his host's further complaints about the recurring brush fires, which frightened the cattle into abandoning their regular pastures for places where they were vulnerable to bears. Ordinarily, babbling brooks and streamlets coursed through Sinclair's immense property. But, as Sandels jotted in his journal, this was a drought year which left the soil cracked and uncomfortable for travelers, and he saw very few flowers on either Sutter's lands or on Sinclair's ranch.[34]

The name "Ranch of the Pass" referred to a natural ford on the American River near today's H Street Bridge that allowed access to Sutter's New Helvetia land grant settlement, and the vast open lands south of the river. Described in modern terms, the Rancho del Paso extended from Northgate Boulevard in Sacramento, east to Manzanita Avenue / Fair Oaks Boulevard in Carmichael, and south from its American River boundary where Cal Expo now stands to a few miles north of McClellan Air Force Base.[35] It was an impressively large landholding and its resident owner/manager was unmarried.

During the previous two years a handful of single immigrant American women had passed through Sutter's trading post. Perhaps one or more had "set her cap" for John Sinclair, who would naturally, as an associate and close neighbor of Captain Sutter, have met most visitors and new immigrant groups. For instance—whether John knew this or not—just the year before Mrs. Vardamon Bennett, lately arrived from Oregon Territory with four marriage-aged daughters, had bragged to a sea captain's wife that he would be her son-in-law. But as 1844 dawned John Sinclair was finally ready to marry and he fell for young Mary Eyre, an attractive flaxen-haired blonde whose pale complexion and slender form gave the deceptive impression of porcelain-doll frailty.[36]

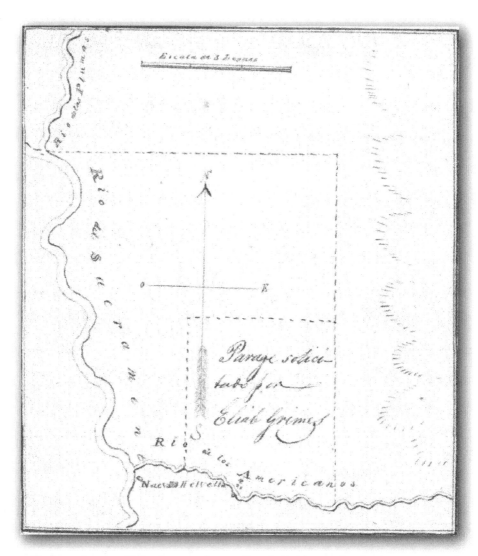

The map-sketch, called a diseño, submitted by Eliab Grimes when he petitioned for the Rancho del Paso land grant in 1844. At lower left is Sutter's Fort, situated on the southern portion of John Sutter's Nueva Helvetia land grant. —Author's collection.

*Chapter 3*

## TO BE MY WEDDED SPOUSE

The immediate obstacle to John and Mary's budding romance was Captain John Sutter himself, who knew better than to allow an unattached young woman to live at his settlement amidst the hard-bitten frontiersmen and adventurers who constituted his employees. Around this time Sutter was preparing his schooner, the *Sacramento*, for a voyage to the Napa Embarcadero to pick up a quantity of limestone from Nicolas Higuera, the owner of Rancho Entre Napa.

Higuera's ranch was ten or so miles south of George Yount's property. Sutter gave passage on the *Sacramento* to Elizabeth Yount, her sister Frances Yount Vines and the Vines family; Joseph Chiles, Billy Baldridge, and Mary Eyre. Did John impulsively board the vessel to press his suit for Mary's hand, thereby joining the happy Yount family reunion, or woo Mary with later visits, pushing his horse to a full gallop? It's impossible to know. They were married in the Napa Valley in 1844, after Mary asked for, and Billy Baldridge granted, his permission, but record of the exact date and place, or who solemnized their vows, has been lost. [37]

Finding someone to perform the marriage ceremony was another obstacle. In Mexican California, where there was no separation of church and state, the priesthood adamantly refused to marry non-Catholics (or a Catholic to a non-believer) and the government only recognized those marriages which were blessed by the priesthood. On paper at least, under the requirements of his Mexican citizenship, John Sinclair was a declared Catholic, whereas Mary's English family were Protestants. This dual-faith situation, or non-faith in the eyes of the Church, also became problematic for other couples wishing to marry as the numbers of American immigrants increased, most of whom were Protestant—but there was no Protestant clergy in California until 1846. An accepted alternative was to be married by a local *alcalde* (a judge), but even here native-born alcaldes generally declined to officiate at mixed-faith marriages. For some years past John Sutter, by enlarging upon the broad powers granted him by Governor Alvarado, had indeed wed a few couples inside his fort, drawing ire from officialdom as to the legality of these unions apparently only on those occasions when one or both of the participants were members of the Catholic Church. Nevertheless, Sutter had no jurisdiction beyond his own domain.[38]

The Sinclairs were married in the Napa Valley, in a year when no towns yet existed there; and therefore no city recorder to document the nuptials. Under Mexican rule the present-day counties of Napa and Sonoma were combined into one political jurisdiction, the District of Sonoma. Jacob Primer Leese, an American, and the brother-in-law of General Mariano Vallejo, was alcalde of the Sonoma District 1844-45. Naturalized as a Mexican citizen in 1836, Leese was a strong individualist not easily cowed by edicts he deemed irrelevant. An important, influential trader in early California, Leese was known to put his business interests above other considerations. One of his lucrative business relationships was with Eliab Grimes, and he knew John Sinclair as well.[39] There is, however, no evidence that Leese officiated at the Sinclair's marriage.

Given the limited options they faced in 1844, it is quite plausible that John and Mary composed and signed a contract of marriage which declared their intention to cohabit as man and wife, then exchanged simple vows in front of witnesses who also affixed their signatures to the document, without an officiator present. If so, they were not the only couple to exercise this method of do-it-yourself wedlock. The most infamous example of this practice was the September 1845 marriage of American citizens Isaac Graham and Catherine Bennett. Infamous, that is, when the couple separated and a pitched battle ensued over custody of their children. In her petition to the court, Catherine claimed that Isaac had no right to the children because the marriage itself, unsanctioned by clergy of any sort, and unrecognized under Mexican law, was invalid. She lost, though. The Graham-Bennett marriage was adjudged valid by the California Supreme Court (*Graham v. Bennett*, 1852), based on Judge Heydenfeldt's opinion that, "Marriage is regarded as a civil contract and no form is necessary for its solemnization...If it take place between parties able to contract, an open avowal of the intention, and an assumption of the relative duties which it imposes in each other, is sufficient to render it valid and binding."

John and Mary's wedding likely took place on George Yount's ranch, where Mary was the live-in guest of her friend Elizabeth Yount. Mary's seventeenth birthday was on March 29. Chances are that the wedding date was sometime in April, a surmise based on two vague clues.

The first clue is in the reports submitted by explorer Lieutenant John Charles Frémont. On March 6, 1844, Frémont, his guide Kit Carson, and the forward sections of his company of Topographical Engineers rode past Sinclair's home on their way to Sutter's Fort. Famished and exhausted after their near-fatal trek over the Sierra, Frémont and his followers remained encamped in the vicinity of the fort until March 22, to rest themselves and their bedraggled mounts while Sutter's skilled craftsmen manufactured saddles and bridles to replace those lost in the mountains. As far as we can tell, Frémont and Sinclair initially met on March 8, when Sutter hosted a banquet to honor the new arrivals. During his visit Frémont jotted down his observations of Sutter's thriving establishment. He noted the young Indian girls he saw who were to receive training for a future woolen factory at the fort, but were instead watering the garden. We can only wish that Frémont's journal entry had been just as specific about John, instead of writing, "Mr. Sinclair, from whom I experienced much kindness during my stay, is settled a few miles distant on the Rio de los Americanos." Frémont did not mention a wife.[40] If John Sinclair had been newly married at that time one might suppose that Frémont, himself a happily married man, would have mentioned his kind benefactor's recent marital happiness. Or, unwilling to record such a personal comment, would at the very least have noted the presence of an Anglo lady living so close to the fort—a circumstance sure to lift the hearts of his men, who hadn't seen a white woman for five months.

The second clue is from Mary's own words, recorded nearly fifty years later. In 1892, she told members of a Boston pioneer society that she had been "the only lady among the pioneers at Sutter's Fort for about a year." [41]

Besides Mary, the first white women at Sutter's Fort in 1844 were Elizabeth (Mrs. John) Townsend and Ellen Murphy, who had set out on horseback to seek help for the rest of the fifty-odd member Stephens-Murphy-Townsend Party stranded in the mountains. These two women, and four men, rode into Sutter's Fort on December 10. In December of the previous year, Mary Sinclair was still traveling with the Walker-Chiles wagon train; and although Ellen Murphy and Elizabeth Townsend stayed at Sutter's Fort for some weeks, neither woman settled in the area. It is more plausible that Mary counted March 1845 as the end of her near-year as the only lady among the pioneers, which supports the guess that her wedding had been in the month of April. In March 1845, six more ladies, and their children, arrived at Sutter's Fort, having been rescued from a snowed-in winter camp on the Yuba River. Two of the six women established homes in the general vicinity of Sutter's trading post. They were Sarah Armstrong Montgomery, two years older than Mary Sinclair, married to gunsmith Allen Montgomery, and Mary Bolger Murphy, long-married to Martin Murphy, Junior. Mary Murphy was the mother of four young sons and an infant daughter born at the Yuba River campsite. Allen and Sarah Montgomery built a cabin not far from Sutter's Fort, and the Murphy family settled twenty miles south on acreage near the Cosumnes River. [42]

John and Mary had met the little band of horse riders in December 1844, before they entered Sutter's gates. No doubt the Sinclairs were amazed and enthralled to learn from them that their wagon train had followed the faint tracks of the 1843 Walker-Chiles Party wagons—Mary's company—to the Humboldt Sink, where the tracks continued southward. But at the Sink, the Stephens-Murphy-Townsend Party made the decision to head due west. In so doing, they opened the first practical wagon route to California, later known as the Truckee Route. By mid-November the company was camped at high altitude, where they faced another hard decision. Here, the Truckee River veered south toward its origin in Lake Tahoe, but Truckee Creek flowed west, and looked to be a more promising route for the wagons. Snow was falling. They decided that six strong young people, on horseback, should follow the main stream while the wagons continued toward the Sierra summit. Murphy senior's daughter Ellen, her brothers John and Daniel, Elizabeth Townsend, and two hired men agreed to go. Hopefully, the riders would reach Sutter's Fort first and send help.

The riders followed the Truckee River to Lake Tahoe, and then rode along the lake's western shore, where they ascended another stream which took them up and over the rim. From there they descended out of the snow to the Rubicon River, and followed it to the middle branch of the American River. The rugged terrain was dangerous and exhausting. Riding through steep, narrow canyons, they eventually worked their way to the north side of the river's main branch and down, at last chancing to find the Sinclair's home. Along the way the group had now and then made meals of the cattle they saw roaming the foothills, and were guilt-stricken when they learned that the cattle belonged to John and Mary. They offered to pay for the animals, but the Sinclairs would have none of it. After resting for a time, the little party rode on to Sutter's Fort. [43]

The newlywed Sinclairs had taken up residence in John's bachelor adobe in the southern part of the Rancho del Paso. Here clusters of giant oak trees, bright yellow wild mustard, and the brilliant orange-gold of native poppies dotted the multi-green shaded grasses in a gently rolling landscape. The land provided abundant grazing for cattle, horses, hogs and sheep; John would later acquire a valued Merino ram for stockbreeding. The couple probably expected to lead quiet country lives but were about to be swept up in a series of tumultuous events, the first being a revolution to oust Governor Micheltorena.

*Chapter 4*

## SCHEMERS AND CONQUERORS

Manuel Micheltorena, who had arrived from Mexico to assume his duties as governor of the province almost two years earlier, had so managed to incite the antagonism of his subjects that by the fall of 1844, General José Castro and former California governor Juan Alvarado were plotting to drive him out of the country. John Sutter agreed to mount a military campaign to assist Micheltorena. He organized and drilled an army of volunteers inside the walls of his compound, with others—settlers of diverse national origin—expected to join up along the brigade's route. Sinclair was among the troops as one of two aide-de-camps when Captain Sutter's makeshift army marched out of the fort on January 1, 1845, with banners flying. Yet it wasn't long before resolve faltered in the minds of Sutter's followers: driving rains, inadequate clothing, poor rations, and dissention in the ranks all contributed to a dismal journey. South of Santa Barbara, whole squadrons began to defect.

During the campaign Sutter intermittently sent long letters of instructions and commentary to Pierson B. Reading, who was holding down the fort in Sutter's absence. In the correspondence dated January 15, Sutter first tells Reading that "Mr. Sinclair do his duty very well as Aide de Camp," [*sic*] and then complained that he had just received anxious letters from Sinclair's partner Captain Eliab Grimes, addressed to him and John Sinclair. These were hand-delivered by Joel Dedmond, who was not a member of Sutter's army. Dedmond, whom Sutter called a "mean, undermining fellow," and "a neighbor I don't like to have," owned the Rancho San Juan directly east of the Rancho del Paso. Sutter's fractured English could barely express his indignation at what he believed were Dedmond's unscrupulous tactics. Why, Dedmond had purposely "worked by old Grimes to try and get Sinclair out of his situation." (What benefit this would be to Joel Dedmond is unclear.) We don't know what Eliab Grimes' letters said, but we might assume that John Sinclair shared Sutter's low opinion of Dedmond's character, because John remained with the troops.

A month later, though, as Sutter's and Micheltorena's combined forces neared Mission San Buenaventura, Sinclair was fed up enough with the overall operation to have second thoughts. On or about February 16 he turned about and headed home to Mary, taking with him a letter from Sutter to Reading dated February 15, as well as additional verbal instructions. From the tone of this letter Sutter appears quite unperturbed by Sinclair's decision. Only years later did Sutter bitterly characterize John's defection as an act of cowardice.

The campaign continued. Farther south at Los Angeles, the rebels triumphed. John Sutter was captured but later released. Micheltorena surrendered, and was deported to Mexico. Pio Pico, a life-long resident of southern California, was sworn in as the new governor and promptly moved the capital to Los Angeles.[44] *Comandante General* José Castro returned to his home in Monterey, no doubt thinking himself capable of crushing any future political upheaval that involved meddling foreign upstarts. A year later Castro would find himself embroiled with yet more dangerous foreigners, and a far more competent military adversary.

## The Interim
Except for some local Indian troubles, during which John Sinclair may or may not have joined Sutter's retaliatory riders, peace prevailed for

several months until the influx of Americans in covered wagons once more caused suspicion to swell in the hearts of Mexican officials.

On September 27, the first of several segments of the 1845 immigration arrived at Sutter's Fort. More appeared throughout most of October. Altogether they numbered some 250 individuals, the largest body of overlanders from the United States so far. Among the immigrants were thirteen young single men riding pack mules, captained by friends William Todd and William Swasey, and the wagons of the large John Grigsby-William Ide Party, bringing women and children. John Sutter hired some of the men for various jobs; others replenished their provisions and moved on to settle elsewhere. The emigrant trail wound along the outskirts of the Rancho del Paso, so it is reasonable to suppose that John and Mary met several, if not most, of the newcomers as the riders and wagons approached the ford to cross the American River.

On October 21, the first warning bell rang. Captain Sutter received a dispatch from the province's local Mexican government telling him to stop the immigration—as if, by some obscure logic, one man had the god-like power to do so. The message was not for people like the Sinclairs, who were naturalized Mexican citizens. It was for the feared *Americanos*, who—from Mexico City's point of view—had stolen Texas from the Republic of Mexico some years past; and who were, despite warnings, courting outright war with their insistence on annexing Texas to the United States. Sutter held a meeting with the immigrants to read aloud California Governor Pio Pico's decree, and assure them of his help.[45] When a week passed with no new threats or overt action, the new arrivees, maybe a bit shaken yet determined to stay—and in fact in no condition to leave—set about the tasks of establishing new homes and livelihoods in California. John Grigsby, for instance, took his family to the Napa Valley, where he was hired by the Sinclairs' friend George Yount.

The *New Helvetia Diary,* the logbook of daily activities at Sutter's Fort which records these September-October events, makes no mention of John Sinclair until November 30, when he came to the fort to collect some stock. The Sutter-Sinclair friendship had hit another rough patch earlier, with Sutter complaining in writing to prominent Monterey merchant and U.S. Consul Thomas O. Larkin that his "bad neighbors" John Sinclair, Theodore Cordua and Dr. John Marsh had unjustly taken a good deal of furs from Sutter's trappers, exchanging them for articles the trappers wanted when Sutter himself had none of these goods on hand. Probably this was a mixture of high mischief and simple opportunity when Marsh, Cordua and Sinclair—who had all defected from the Micheltorena campaign at one point or another—returned to the Sacramento Valley weeks ahead of Sutter, to learn that the season's fur catch was still laying about because head trapper Pierson Reading had kept his men at home to garrison the fort.[46]

The fur-appropriating incident, which occurred not long after Sinclair's withdrawal from Sutter's military operation to aid Micheltorena, apparently dampened the friendship for a time. Whatever their personal grudges, though, individuals who lived in relative isolation from the majority of the province's population could ill-afford to remain at odds with each other. Cordial relations resumed.

In December 1845, Sutter and Lansford Hastings, a young Ohio lawyer and wagon train captain during 1842-43, "went up to Mr. Sinclair's" for a visit, most likely on business. There was time for socializing, too. On Thursday, January 29, 1846, Sarah Montgomery, erstwhile member of the Stephens-Murphy-Townsend Party, threw the first quilting bee in the entire inland district. There is every reason to believe that Mary Sinclair attended this event because every woman living within several miles around went, and so did their husbands. The quilting bee was a day-long session of stitching, laughter and friendly chatter for the ladies. For the men, it was an opportunity for a few hours of relaxation in which to exchange news and opinions.

To everyone's surprise, brevet captain John Frémont and some of his men had reappeared at Sutter's Fort December 10, 1845, but shortly were off southward to find a detachment of his Topographical Corps, which was being guided into California by Joseph Walker. Returning from that fruitless foray, Frémont departed for the coast in Sutter's launch on January 19. Two months later he was again camped on the American River with his company, preparatory to heading north. The skies were alternately cold and cloudy, or filled with rain. People came and went from Sutter's Fort, a few of whom crossed the river to pay social calls on the Sinclairs. On May 31, 1846, Eliab Grimes arrived at Sutter's landing on the Sacramento River.[47] It was not the honorable old sea captain's first or last visit to the Rancho del Paso, but this time he would witness the unfolding of two major events: the Bear Flag Revolt, and the American conquest of California.

Surely Captain Grimes was immediately apprised of the fomenting turmoil among the American settlers, many of whom had just arrived in California the previous fall. Rumors were rife that General José Castro now intended to forcibly expel them from the province; and further, that he had sent Lieutenant Francisco Arce to Sonoma to round up a herd of almost two hundred government horses for just that purpose. On June 8 they were informed that the herd had just crossed the Sacramento River at Knight's Landing, and were headed south for Castro's Santa Clara headquarters. Frightened, angry, and agitated, some of the settlers were milling about Sutter's Fort while others had ridden north to confer with Captain John Frémont, who was camped at the Sutter Buttes with his command of sixty armed, irregular soldiers. Frémont's recent return from Oregon, where he had gone after being told by a suspicious José Castro to leave California, emboldened the settlers. When Frémont refused to publicly lead them, a few took matters into their own hands.

## The Bear Flaggers and the American Invasion

On the morning of June 10, a band of twelve or so settlers led by Ezekiel Merritt, formerly one of Sutter's fur trappers, confiscated Lieutenant Acre's horses from the corrals of Martin Murphy Junior's ranch on the Cosumnes River, where the herd had been penned for the night. Driving the horses north to Frémont's camp, Merritt and his fellow ruffians stopped at Sutter's Fort en route, where they greatly alarmed those who had not joined the fray, and who felt this action—either blatant horse thievery or an act of war—was certain to bring reprisals from Mexican officialdom. Instead, on June 16, Sutter and his neighbors were astonished to learn that an even larger group, again led by Merritt, had captured the little town of Sonoma, declared California an independent republic, and hoisted, on the plaza's flagpole, a hastily-stitched flag embellished with a painted grizzly bear and a single red star. Several men from the 1845 immigration were involved, with two of them taking conspicuous roles. William Todd of the Swasey-Todd Party designed and fashioned the Bear Flag; William Ide, of the Grigsby-Ide Party, was the president of the new republic while it lasted. More, the rebels had taken prisoners: Mariano Vallejo, *comandante general* of the Sonoma District; his secretary Victor Prudon, his brother Salvador, and his brother-in-law Jacob Leese.

Meantime, Captain Frémont had moved his camp sixty miles south to the vicinity of the Sinclair's front door. Here, the Bear Flaggers turned over their captives to Frémont, who ordered that they be jailed in Sutter's Fort, and was quite angry when Sutter treated them kindly. It might even be that John Sinclair occasionally joined in at the frequent games of chess and cards that Sutter enjoyed with his "guests." No record of Frémont's interaction with the Sinclairs survives, but no doubt he conferred at length with Eliab Grimes. In February 1847, having been named governor of California by Commodore Robert Stockton, John Frémont appointed Grimes, and six other prominent men, to his Legislative Council. The other appointees were U.S. Consul Thomas O. Larkin, San Diego rancher Juan Bandini, retired Mexican army captain Santiago Arguello, former California governor Juan Alvarado, influential Scotsman David Spence, and Mariano Vallejo. Grimes, then in Hawaii, was expected to return shortly.[48] As things turned out, this council disbanded after Frémont was arrested for mutiny and insubordination by his superior officer, General Stephen Watts Kearny.

Through all of the drama surrounding the Bear Flag Revolt June 14-18 and the troubling incidents that followed, no one in California knew that the United States had officially declared war on Mexico the previous May 13, over the contested Texas boundary. While the boundary issue was the stated objective for war, months earlier President James Polk had realized that the dispute could be used as leverage in his determination to acquire California. John Sinclair did not participate in the Bear Flag Revolt, and the California Republic lasted less than a month. On July 7, 1846, Commodore John Drake Sloat, commanding the U.S. Navy's Pacific Squadron, seized the port of Monterey and raised the American flag over the customhouse. The Bear Flag had been trumped by the Stars and Stripes, and the Mexican-American War had come to California soil.

Within days, Commodore Robert Field Stockton replaced the ailing Sloat. Captain John Frémont immediately set about organizing the California Battalion, recruiting almost all of the Bear Flaggers. He commandeered Sutter's Fort as an operations base, putting his own man, Lieutenant Edward Kern, in charge of what he renamed Fort Sacramento, thus relegating John Sutter to second place in his own establishment. The Sinclairs left no record of how all this turmoil affected them. Still, we can safely imagine that several situational changes in such a short time produced certain anxieties. Frémont and his growing army were again camped on the Rancho del Paso on July 10, 1846, preparing to leave for Monterey. Except for the military men who arrived in California by land and sea under official order, service in the Mexican-American War was voluntary. Sinclair chose to remain at his ranch, supplying the California Battalion with horses and cattle for which, after exhausting other channels for payment, he later filed a claim against the American government for $450.[49]

On September 15, 1846, with the American conquest still incomplete, Commodore Stockton announced that the inhabitants of each settlement in California were entitled to elect their own magistrates and to replace, if they chose, those who had been appointed. Accordingly, on September 28, the few male settlers still in the environs of Sutter's Fort met to elect a Sacramento District *alcalde*, an important civil post in the Mexican political system that combined, into one office, the roles of judge, justice of the peace, mayor, recorder-registrar, and other executive duties as might arise. Of the three candidates John Sinclair, Jared Sheldon and John Sutter, Sinclair resoundingly won with fifteen votes out of the twenty-four cast.

*Chapter 5*

INCOMING SETTLERS: DISASTER,
AND RECOVERY

More would-be California settlers were on the way. That fall an estimated 1,500 immigrants, many of whom would join various military organizations for wartime duty, traversed portions of the Rancho del Paso on the trail to Sutter's Fort, that well-known haven for truly destitute overlanders who had lost family, possessions and teams, as well as the more fortunate who were only trail-worn and weary. It was, by far, the largest influx of overlanders to date.

The first to arrive was a small party of mule-mounted men led by Kentucky journalist Edwin Bryant. Riding south from William Johnson's rustic residence on the Bear River, Bryant and his companions passed through large oak groves where they frequently saw abundant herds of deer and antelope, reaching the bottomlands of the Rancho del Paso at four o'clock in the afternoon on September 1, 1846. Here they encountered John Sinclair, with a number of whooping, hat-waving Indian *vaqueros,* threshing wheat frontier-style: trampling the grain into great piles of chaff and wheat berry by stampeding a herd of twenty-five or so horses in circles inside a corral filled with wheat heads. Bryant noted that ditches five feet deep and four to five feet wide, instead of fences, separated the wheat fields from large herds of cattle and horses, and learned that John expected a crop of three thousand bushels. Leaving John to his work, Bryant was searching for the ford across the American River in order to proceed on to Sutter's Fort when he saw Mary engrossed in giving instructions to her female servants. "I saw a lady of a graceful though fragile figure, dressed in the costume of our own countrywomen," he wrote in his journal. "Her pale and delicate, but handsome and expressive countenance indicated much surprise, produced by my sudden and unexpected salutation. But...she replied to my inquiry [for directions] in vernacular English, and the sounds of her voice...and her civilized appearance, were highly pleasing. This lady, I presume, was Mrs. Sinclair, but I never saw her afterwards."

In describing the Sinclair's residence, Bryant noted that "the dwelling-house and out-houses...are all constructed after American models, and present a most comfortable and neat appearance." [50] Bryant's description suggests either wood construction, or adobe brickwork in a style similar to Massachusetts-born Thomas Larkin's Monterey residence, built in 1835 of adobe blocks with a hipped, wood-shaked roof. John's bachelor dwelling, as seen by sailor John Yates in 1842, was a modest structure. But in August 1844—the year of his marriage—he and Eliab Grimes received 3,625 feet of board lumber, and expected more, from merchant Thomas Larkin to "commence building." Grimes's letter to Larkin, which obviously follows an earlier personal discussion, doesn't specify what the lumber was to be used for. Possibly, it was for an addition to John's house that relegated the original rooms to kitchen and storage, with a wooden or enlarged adobe brick section serving as living quarters. [51] Whatever its ultimate construction and appearance, Edwin Bryant was favorably impressed.

Another diarist was not. Coming along the same route six weeks later with his traveling companion, Swiss immigrant Heinrich Lienhard opined that the house was "plain, even primitive [but] delightfully situated near the bank of the American Fork at a point where the river was unusually smooth and broad." Lienhard did, though, appreciate the wild blackberries he found along the road, and remarked that "Two attractive white women were leaning out of an open window, watching us approach. They spoke to us as we drew near, and said the property on which they were living belonged to a Mr. Sinclair, a Scotsman who was justice of the peace. One of the two women who talked to us was his wife."[52] Lienhard did not identify the second attractive lady. Most likely she was Amanda (Mrs. Daniel) Rhoads come to inspect her future home on the Sinclair's ranch-lands, or maybe reputed beauty Sarah (Mrs. Allen) Montgomery, hostess of the previous January's quilting party. Sarah had moved into Sutter's Fort on June 21 when her husband left to join Frémont's California Battalion.

Eliab Grimes returned to his own new residence in Yerba Buena, but throughout September and October the overlanders' wagons kept rolling in.

Among the newcomers were Thomas Foster Rhoads Senior and his wife Elizabeth, Mormons from Illinois. They arrived at Sutter's Fort on October 5, 1846, with their large family of children and grandchildren. Thomas, who soon settled near today's Galt with most of his family, found temporary work with Captain Sutter. Twenty-four-year-old Daniel Rhoads took a job with John Sinclair, officially hired on from November 1 until the harvesting was expected to be complete the following August. His wages were $25 per month, payable in young cattle: cows at the calving at $4 a head and bulls at $3. The Sinclairs also provided Daniel and his wife Amanda with a house to live in—probably sharing their own home for awhile, since there wasn't time to build another before the rains began—and supplied them with meals as part of the employment agreement. In December 1846, John officiated at the marriage of Daniel's eldest sister, Elizabeth Rhoads, to Austrian native Sebastian Keyser, a fur trapper who had traveled west with John Sutter in 1838, and now was part-owner of William Johnson's ranch on the Bear River.[53]

## Desperate Souls

In the New Year peace came to California at last on January 13, 1847, with the signing of the Treaty of Cahuenga at San Fernando. It was not a formal treaty between warring nations, but an informal agreement be-tween rival military forces in which the "insurgent Californians" gave up fighting. This happy news may or may not have reached the Sacramento Valley when a living skeleton supported by two Indians stumbled into an immigrant's shack on the outskirts of the Johnson-Keyser property on January 17, 1847.

The emaciated, half-dead man was William Eddy. He was one of fifteen desperate individuals who had spent an agonizing thirty-three days traversing the snow-packed Sierra on crudely-fashioned snowshoes to find help for the Donner Party, which had been trapped at a small mountain lake since October 31. He reported that sixty-five men, wom-en, and children were still there, in dire circumstances. Of the fourteen people who had accompanied Eddy, only six others were still alive—one man, William Foster, and all five of the women—now prostrate with exhaustion at a pitiable camp some six miles back. The shack belonged to Matthew D. Ritchie, an 1846 immigrant, and it was Ritchie's teenaged daughter Harriet who first saw William Eddy, bursting into tears before helping him into the house and a bed. Harriet roused the neighbors and soon four men with packs set out by the light of the moon. The next day men on horses brought the other six survivors in, starved and tattered to near-nakedness. From his bed Eddy dictated a letter to Alcalde John Sinclair. A runner—forced to go on foot because the recent rains had transformed the valley into half-lake and half-quagmire that would have bogged down a horse—took it to Rancho del Paso.

Finding that Sinclair was away at Yerba Buena (renamed San Francisco by January's end), the runner gave the letter to Mary, whose first re-sponse was to send him back with a load of petticoats and chemises for the five women. Next, Mary appealed to Edward Kern, still the com-manding officer at Fort Sacramento. Kern gathered together the few men at the settlement who had not been drawn into war service and asked for volunteers to rescue the entrapped immigrants, offering the princely sum of three dollars per day to be paid by the government. Only three men stepped forward. Three wasn't enough, and when Sinclair returned days later to read Eddy's letter himself, he and John Sutter agreed to become personally responsible for the wages Kern had stipulated.[54] On January 29, 1847, Alcalde Sinclair composed a harrowing narrative addressed to Alcalde Washington Allon Bartlett of Yerba Buena, which was taken downriver on John Sutter's launch to inform bay area residents, and solicit donations to the cause.* Then—because the land was still flooded— on January 30 he set out on foot for Johnson's to interview Eddy and the others, arriving there on Sunday, January 31. What Sinclair learned from Foster, Eddy, and the five women was yet more chilling than the frozen peaks.

The flour and other provisions piled on seven pack mules that John Sutter had sent to the company's aid the previous September, before they had even entered the mountains, had been consumed long ago. The cattle that would have sustained them had been killed by Indians in the Nevada desert, or irretrievably lost beneath mountain snowdrifts. Men, women and children were holed up in inadequate shelters in sub-zero weather, reduced to eating boiled ox hides. Teamster Baylis Williams had died the day before the snow-shoe party (later immortalized as "The Forlorn Hope" by writer C. F. McGlashan), left the lake. Two more men were presumed dead after attempting, in the midst of a storm, to reach the other faction of the company stalled eight miles back at Alder Creek; and indications were that more individuals would shortly perish from starvation and exposure. Most horrifying of all were the confessions by the surviving snow-shoers that they had resorted to cannibalizing their dead companions to stay alive themselves.[55]

Immediately upon arriving at Johnson's ranch, John Sinclair asked that all the horses scattered about the neighborhood be rounded up, in order to select the best for either carrying the rescuers as far as practical or for packing their provisions. Obtaining these, said Matthew Ritchie, was considerable trouble. Next, Sinclair supervised the rigging of make-do

---

* See Appendix for the complete letter. It was printed in the *New York Weekly Tribune* on September 18, 1847, and the *Ohio Observer* October 16, 1847. Sinclair's second and longer report dated February 1847 was published in Edwin Bryant's *What I Saw in California* in 1848.

saddles from cow hides, and undoubtedly assisted with the hurried slicing and jerking of the five or six butchered beef that William Johnson provided.

Elsewhere, volunteers and equipment were being gathered from San Jose, Sonoma, and Yerba Buena. James Reed, who had been banished from the Donner Party while they were still traveling along the Humboldt River, and who had tried and failed to reach them months earlier, raised funds for supplies. It took time. While Reed and others in the Bay Area were still making preparations, the first band of rescuers, which included Sinclair's employee Daniel Rhoads and his brother John Rhoads, mustered for departure from Johnson's. On Thursday February 4, Sinclair called the rescue party together and delivered a rousing speech of encouragement (a "thrilling little address," said rescue team member George Tucker). They started out the next day, reaching the lake cabins on February 19, 1847. John returned home, probably on February 8 after a heated exchange the night before with Edward Kern, who had come up from Sutter's Fort but initially refused to part with some foodstuffs that John believed was intended for the stranded immigrants. Once back on his ranch, he and Captain Sutter set about organizing more supplies and horses for the rescue effort.[56]

Counting the seven surviving adults of William Eddy's group, and the others brought out of the mountains by three successive relief parties, slightly over half of the Donner Party reached safety by the end of March. The rest perished. Five now remained in the mountains: three adults and one young boy, so near death as to be unable to rise from their beds when last seen; and Tamzen Donner, who adamantly refused to leave her dying husband George. Another rescue party assembled and got as far as Bear Valley, but turned back when the winds of an incoming major storm began howling through the trees. By the time the weather cleared in early April, those five still at the lake camps were assumed to be dead.

Still, the immigrant's wagons had contained many valuable items that might be ruined if left to the elements. In a letter dated April 10, 1847, Alcalde John Sinclair authorized former mountain man and Bear

Flag Revolt participant William O. Fallon to lead a salvage expedition. To everyone's amazement, this group also brought in a last survivor, Louis Keseburg. The following month, in a document dated May 5, 1847, Sinclair granted salvage rights to John Rhoads and his team for one-half of Jacob and George Donners' property still remaining at the lake. The other half was to be used for the benefit of the Donners' heirs. On June 2, 1847 Sinclair held an auction at the Rancho del Paso for the benefit of the Donner children, selling the recovered goods which had belonged to their parents. Additional administrative duties stretched over several weeks as John either conferred in person with adult survivors, or composed and received a number of letters regarding the disposition of their own or their dead family members' salvaged property.[57]

The refugees were taken to Sutter's Fort to recover and convalesce, the only close-at-hand facility capable of providing shelter and sustenance for so many. Even so, because the fort contained few bedrooms—and a number of the 1846 immigrants were still residing in the additional mud-brick living quarters erected outside the walls the previous year—there weren't enough beds for everyone. Some of the survivors were placed with nearby settlers. John and Mary Sinclair took in the James Reed family, which kindled a close friendship between the two couples. Margret Reed, with her children Virginia and Jimmy, were among the first survivors to reach safety. James struggled on with the second rescue team through thirty-foot snowdrifts and storms, to bring out the couple's two other children and any others who might still be alive. John and Mary tried to lift everyone's spirits with hopeful thoughts for Reed's success, but Margret was consumed with dread. Unable to sleep at night, she stood in the Sinclair's doorway for hours staring out toward the distant peaks. Margret's fears were justified...but in the end dispelled. After enduring a blizzard, and temporary snow blindness, James Reed, with eight-year-old Martha (nicknamed Patty) and three-year-old Tommy, rejoined the others at the Sinclair's home about mid-March.[58]

Soon afterward, the very young orphaned daughters of George and Tamzen Donner—Frances, Georgia and Eliza—all aged six and under, were brought in with the third relief effort. Traveling down from Johnson's ranch toward Sutter's Fort, it was too dark to cross the river by the time they reached the Sinclair's residence. Eliza Donner never forgot Mary's hospitable reception when the house was already crowded, and all the beds and blankets were in use. Mary loosened the rag-carpet from one corner of the room, laid down fresh straw on the floor, tucked the little girls away on the straw, and pulled the carpet over them in place of quilts. For supper, Mary gave them what they hadn't tasted in months, a delicious repast of fresh bread and milk, and more of the same the next day before they were canoed across the river to the fort.[59]

Although the Mexican-American War still raged on in Mexico, the cessation of hostilities inside California, reinforced by the continued presence of American troops, brought a sense of relief and rejuvenation. Romance was in the air. On March 4, 1847, John married Sarah Rhoads and William Daylor. On March 14, he married Catherine Rhoads to Daylor's friend Jared Sheldon. Both teenaged brides were the younger sisters of Sinclair's ranch hand, Daniel Rhoads. Both bridegrooms, who shared ownership of the Rancho Omochumney on the Cosumnes River, were Captain John Sutter's former employees.[60]

Sutter, Sinclair, and many others kindly did what they could to help the Donner Party survivors heal and start fresh lives, but the drama surrounding their rescue wasn't completely over. The men who had brought Louis Keseburg in from the mountains in April stirred up best-forgotten memories by spreading tales of the deplorable conditions they had found at the lake camps, and they accused Keseburg of murdering Tamzen Donner. To refute this charge Keseburg brought action for defamation of character, asking $1,000 in damages. The trial began May 5, Alcalde Sinclair presiding as judge. The verdict was ambiguous: the jury found for the plaintiff, but only awarded one dollar. Two weeks later, Judge Sinclair held court in a matter which doubtless brought more satisfaction to the locals. Two horse thieves, who had also absconded with an immigrant's Indian servant and some pistols, were found guilty and transported downriver in Sutter's launch to San Francisco for imprisonment.[61]

**New Day, New Hopes, New Life**

While this unpleasantness was going on John Sinclair officiated at still more weddings, most of them the start of a new life for Donner Party survivors, all solemnized within the walls of Sutter's Fort. On May 16, dark-eyed beauty Mary Ann Graves, "the belle of the Donner Party," wed Edward Gantt Pyle, Jr., an overland immigrant of 1846 who had carried supplies to the first rescue party. On June 1, orphaned Elitha Donner, just fourteen, married another who had provided essential services to the rescue effort: twenty-five-year-old Perry McCoon, a long-time employee of John Sutter. Survivor Dorothea Wolfinger, whose husband had been killed in the Nevada desert by one of the company's teamsters, exchanged vows on June 20 with George Zins, an 1846 immigrant and fellow German. A few friends and neighbors were on hand to celebrate a double wedding on Thursday, June 24. Widowed Harriet Murphy Pike, whose husband William had died from an accidental gun discharge before the Donner Party reached the lake, was joined in wedlock with tall, handsome Michael Nye, a member of the 1841 Bidwell-Bartleson Party. At the same time, possibly in the same ceremony, Harriet's teenaged sister Mary Murphy married the considerably older Bear River rancher, William Johnson.

Even forty-one-year-old, life-long bachelor John Yates, the captain of Sutter's schooner, jumped on the matrimonial bandwagon May 11 by taking as his wife Elisa Booth, the sixteen-year-old daughter of an English family who had come west with the 1846 wagon trains.[62]

And, while these weddings were taking place, the Sinclairs were preparing to embark on a new life phase as well, that of proud parents. Mary might have realized her condition while the Reeds were still residing on the Rancho del Paso, or they were later told in correspondence now lost, because in a letter to James Reed at San Jose dated June 23, 1847, John's jocular comments make it clear that James and Margret already knew of the coming birth: "What Mrs. Reed means by being ready to come up at any time I do not know but presume there is some plot between her and a certain lady who, as Shakespeare has it, 'rounds apace' and grows exceedingly lusty." In June, then, Mary's slim figure was expanding. "Lusty," another word John borrowed from a Shakespearean drama, meant that the mother-to-be was strong and healthy. Apparently, the Sinclairs were quite fond of the Reed's youngest daughter. John ended the above letter with a playful admonition to Margret: "Tell Mrs. Reed to kiss Martha for me and drop calling her 'Pat' as we are informed that St. Patrick was a gentleman and she is a young lady who I hope will live to be a very old one." [63]

What we don't have is the exact date of the Sinclair baby's birth. Oddly, the New Helvetia Diary—which does note the births of other babies in 1847, white and Indian alike—makes no mention of a child born to the community's magistrate. Neither does it record any visit from the Reeds, who surely would have paid a call on Captain Sutter if they were in the neighborhood. Perhaps, by the time the child was born, James and Margret Reed could not come as promised because of circumstances affecting their own family.

Sometime around the end of September 1847, Mary gave birth to a daughter they named Amelia, presumably in honor of Mary's youngest sister.

*Chapter 6*

CALM BEFORE THE STORM

On the same day that John wrote to the Reeds, June 23, one of Sutter's employees brought word that the Walla Walla Indians, having been released from war duty, were stealing horses from settlers and harassing local Indian villages on their way back to Oregon Territory. Together, Justice Sinclair and Lieutenant Charles Anderson, who had arrived at Fort Sacramento the previous month with a detachment of Jonathan Stevenson's New York Volunteers to replace Edward Kern's command, tried to raise an armed force. However, since not one of the other valleyites showed any inclination to join, the proposed campaign fizzled.[64]

Despite this Indian issue, Sinclair's upbeat letter to James Reed was written in the belief that the Reeds had successfully settled into their new home in San Jose. (Or so he thought; actually the Reed family was still enjoying an extended visit on George Yount's ranch in Napa.) Another reason for his jovial mood was no doubt based on information filtering in from the front lines in Mexico that the war was, hopefully, just about over. American troops still occupied California's coastal areas to preserve the peace, but by the summer of 1847 Sacramento Valley locals were back to their normal lives tending their fields and livestock. According

to Sutter's employee Heinrich Lienhard, Sinclair was the only farmer besides Sutter who shipped out wheat. In late May, again on November 5,
and yet again in mid-December, Sinclair hosted rodeos (cattle-branding
roundups) at the Rancho del Paso. On October 27, John sent eighty-one
cattle hides—two wagon loads—to John Sutter's tannery for processing,
a necessary step to prevent the hides from rotting while being transported
in ship's holds.[65]

Toward the end of summer, savory gossip made the rounds as first
the Booth-Yates marriage and then the Murphy-Johnson union disintegrated. According to the "facts" that passed from mouth-to-mouth,
Yates had only married Elisa Booth to acquire able-bodied male in-
laws to care for his undeveloped ranch on the Feather River. (Either
overly optimistic or just determined, twenty days after his wedding
Yates had duly registered his branding iron and his ear mark with
Alcalde Sinclair.) Later on young Mary Murphy denounced William
Johnson as an abusive, drunken sot. Both brides indignantly charged
that their bridegrooms had refused to part with their previous Indian
"wives." [66]

Indulging in gossip, however, was but a trifling respite to the daily
physical and mental exertion required of farmers and ranchers. In August
a minor miracle occurred, or so it seemed to the locals who toiled from
dawn to dark but were unable to implement desired improvements without the aid of a skilled workforce. About 150 members of the Mormon
Battalion, many of them experienced craftsmen, camped outside the
walls of Sutter's Fort. Having arrived in southern California too late to
fight in the Mexican-American War, they had nonetheless served out
their contractual period of enlistment. Now recently discharged at Los
Angeles, they were traveling northeast on their way home to the Great
Salt Lake when Brigham Young sent word that provisions were low in the
Utah settlements. Better, Young advised, for them to remain in California
awhile longer and find work. John Sutter, who had been forced to put his
many ambitious plans on hold during the wartime military occupation

of his fort, straightaway hired about eighty of them to work on his various projects. Rancher Jared Sheldon hired approximately twenty to help complete a gristmill on his Cosumnes River ranch. John Sinclair, too, hired an unknown number of Mormons for Rancho del Paso; one source estimates as many as twenty-five. Three of them, apparently unskilled laborers, completed their assignment by September 7, when Sutter hired them to work in his coal pit.[67]

Sutter already had a primitive mule-driven gristmill, but he wanted a water-powered, larger-capacity facility, and his other long-cherished wish was to build a sawmill to produce board lumber. The sites for each mill were already chosen. For the gristmill, a place on the American River about six miles east of the fort called Natoma, and for the sawmill, a lovely, wooded little valley known as Coloma on the river's South Fork some forty miles distant. Sutter was so exuberant at this windfall of sorely needed labor that on August 27, 1847, just two days after the Mormon's arrival, he signed a partnership contract with his employee James Marshall, a talented and experienced jack-of-all-trades, to build the sawmill.

The remainder of 1847 passed as usual but small changes, and new faces, were coming to the valley. On October 12 Charles C. Smith, in association with San Francisco merchant and newspaper publisher Samuel Brannan, opened a store in the adobe building outside the fort's south wall that had once served as the bunkhouse for Sutter's Indian *vaqueros*. The 1847 immigration, though much smaller than that of 1846, brought South Carolina-born, French-educated Dr. Victor J. Fourgeaud with his wife and young son, who arrived at Sutter's Fort October 9. Captain Sutter played host to the doctor and his wife the following day, a Sunday. "Received a visit of Dr. Fourgeaud & his Lady, likewise Mr. Sinclair," noted the *New Helvetia Diary,* implying that Mary was also present. The following Wednesday, the doctor and his family departed for San Francisco aboard Sutter's watercraft. Only thirty-one, Dr. Fourgeaud already enjoyed prominence in St. Louis, Missouri, and would soon gain distinction in San Francisco not only for his abilities as a physician, but also as the author of the first long essay on the resources and attractions of California, "Prospects of California," which appeared in the *California Star* April 1, 1848.

Following Dr. Fourgeaud's visit in October, John Sinclair's presence at the fort is not recorded again until December 1, although the fort's logbook does duly note various cattle transactions between Sutter and Sinclair in the intervening weeks. Also noted are Sutter's infrequent visits to the Rancho del Paso, such as the one in mid-December when Captain Sutter "took a ride over to Mr. Sinclair." John and Mary invited Sutter to dine with them on New Year's Day 1848, a private gathering evidently so enjoyable that Sutter stayed until nine o'clock that night.

Double trouble surfaced five days later. Sinclair came to the fort looking for his prized, runaway Merino ram, and to report that his own dogs had destroyed several of his sheep. That same day Mr. Gingery, a stone cutter or millwright working on Sutter's new gristmill, filed a complaint of assault and battery against two merchants, James Coates and Samuel Norris, who had set up shop near Sutter's tannery the previous May. Happily, the Merino ram was found unharmed the next day. The criminal trial, held at Sinclair's rancho on January 7, decided in favor of Mr. Gingery. Judge Sinclair fined the defendants thirty dollars, which was given over to the district's general treasury fund. On January 25, Sinclair meted out justice in another horse stealing complaint.[68]

## A Very Important Matter

In the following weeks, on-and-off heavy rains and the subsequent deep mud-slicks no doubt hindered essential chores on the Rancho del Paso, such as altering hogs and taking delivery of fifty sheep from John Sutter's flock. In just such a downpour on January 28, 1848, James Marshall rode into the fort to meet in secret with Captain Sutter "on very important business," as Sutter so jotted in the logbook, a gross understatement. The matter the two men discussed that evening was an epoch-making event that would shatter the tranquility of all who lived in California; a just-between-us-for-now secret that inevitably slipped out to span the globe.

The strange behind-locked-doors meeting between Sutter and Marshall sparked curious gossip, but John Sinclair, the only magistrate in the sprawling Sacramento District, had more important matters on his mind. Regardless of the fact that the United States military occupied California, the province still operated under Mexican law which had, for administrative purposes, created geopolitical districts. As district alcalde, John's jurisdiction comprised all the territory north of the San Joaquin Delta, and east of the Sacramento River all the way to the Sierra Nevada. On February 7 he brought in a prisoner from the San Joaquin—profane, reckless Bluford K. "Hell-Raising" Thompson—accused of murdering recent immigrant James McKee. Sinclair convened trial two days later and when that jury couldn't agree summoned another, setting a second trial date five days hence. Thompson was acquitted—to the disgust of a few jurors and spectators alike—and prudently decided it was in his best interests to leave the precinct. Thompson's second trial began and ended February 12.[69] On February 14, the day Sutter's teamster Jacob Wittmer returned from delivering food and supplies to the sawmill crew at Coloma, the object of the earlier, mystifying Sutter-Marshall private conversation suddenly became clear.

At the mill camp, Jacob Wittmer had learned of Marshall's January gold discovery and, moreover, had a few samples in his pocket. Wittmer, who liked his drink, strode into C. C. Smith's combination mercantile and *cantina* outside the fort walls and asked for a bottle of brandy. Charles Smith, wearily familiar with Wittmer's drink-now-maybe-pay-later tendencies, demanded to see his money first. Wittmer showed his gold samples to Smith's disbelieving eyes, and repeated what he'd heard at the mill site. Smith confronted Captain Sutter, who couldn't deny Wittmer's story. John Sinclair happened to be at the fort that day, but there is no record that he cornered Sutter with the questions and concerns appropriate to a man in his position. Seemingly more crucial at the moment was the problem of driving oxen across the swollen American River between the two ranches. Four days later it was the obligation to act as judge at yet another trial held at the fort, this time over an altercation between two of Sutter's employees, one of whom found himself again answering to Judge Sinclair a month later for a dispute with someone else.[70]

In fact, full realization of what Marshall's gold discovery might mean sank slowly into the minds of the colony's inhabitants. Smith, of course, sent word to his partner Sam Brannan in San Francisco. Charles Bennett, the courier Captain Sutter dispatched to military governor Colonel Richard Mason's headquarters at Monterey with a request for a pre-emption on the mill site, couldn't resist showing off his pouch of gold samples to other customers at a saloon in Benecia. Sutter himself couldn't resist bragging in a letter to his creditor Mariano Vallejo. Sawmill crew-member Henry Bigler notified those of his Mormon comrades who were working on Sutter's gristmill downstream. By the end of February curious-yet-skeptical locals, and a few of Sutter's employees, had found a reason to amble uphill to Coloma; a trickle at first, swelling to a steadier flow throughout March.

For awhile, John Sinclair was focused on ordinary matters: sheep shearing, delivering hogs and cattle to Sutter, and entertaining. He and Mary hosted a dinner on March 12 with guests John Sutter, Major Pierson Reading, and visiting Santa Barbara resident Alpheus Thompson, a seagoing merchant who traded between China and California. On March 30, Sinclair presided at trial on a charge of horse stealing brought by German immigrant Peter Cadel against Salines (or Salinas), a Frenchman in Sutter's employ who had been known to appropriate other men's horses in the past. He summoned Captain Sutter as a witness.[71]

As March wore to a close, the number of men filtering through Sutter's trading post increased. Their curiosity, perhaps initially piqued by a March 15 back-page, mildly-phrased paragraph in San Francisco's *Californian* about a gold discovery on the American River, was definitely spiraling higher from mouth-to-mouth speculation. At this point, John decided he should investigate for himself.

On Tuesday, April 4, Sinclair and Dr. Henry Bates, the physician whom Sutter had hired during the measles epidemic among the Indians the previous year, started for the mountains. In a few days, long enough for them to search a considerable amount of ground for "color," they were back in time for Sinclair to send a cargo downriver on Sutter's watercraft the following Monday. Two days later, on April 12, the pair departed again for further exploration, returning April 14. Probably on both forays, Sinclair took along a number of his Indian employees. Historian David Lavender states that Sinclair trained his Indian workers by imitating Isaac Humphrey's well-developed mining methods. Humphrey, a veteran of the 1828 Georgia gold rush, was by happenstance in Benecia when Sutter's courier Charles Bennett brandished his gold samples to the patrons at the local saloon. Electrified, Humphrey left for Coloma with all possible haste. There, he introduced the cradle, or rocker, to the California greenhorns. Built of wood with an opening at the top and a series of cleats along its sloping bottom, this contraption utilized the action of water and the weight of gold far faster and more efficiently than a simple pan or basket. Sinclair may have eventually adopted Humphrey's machine; initially, his teams used baskets. In any event, John Sinclair was the first to mine on the North Fork of the American River where, by nineteenth century standards, he found a small fortune in gold.[72]

Sinclair's success is highlighted in Colonel Richard Barnes Mason's official report on the California gold discoveries, dated August 17, 1848. Unstated in the document was the fact that Mason and Sinclair had been communicating by letter since February, concerning various alcalde duties which fell under Mason's authority in the aftermath of the Mexican-American War. As far as we can tell, the two first met in person during the July Fourth 1848 celebrations at Sutter's Fort, when Mason was beginning his tour of the gold fields. Evidently Mason saw Sinclair again afterward, either at the site of Sinclair's gold claim, or at his home or at the fort on July 10, when Mason again stopped at Sutter's on his return to Monterey. Mason's report states, "Mr. Sinclair...employs about 50 Indians on the north fork, not far from its junction with the main stream. He had been engaged about five weeks when I saw him, and up to that time his Indians had used simply closely woven willow baskets. His net proceeds (which I saw) were about $16,000 worth of gold. He showed me the proceeds of his last week's work—fourteen pounds avoirdupois of clean-washed gold." Colonel Mason included a specimen taken from Sinclair's gold claim, along with twelve more obtained from other sites, with the report he sent to Washington, D.C.[73]

John Sinclair also sent some samples to his friend Robert C. Wyllie, in 1848 the Hawaiian Kingdom's Minister for Foreign Affairs. Through the ineptness of the messenger, a Mr. Suwerkrop, Wyllie never received the samples but thanked Sinclair anyway for his thoughtfulness at sending them.[74]

In his memoir, Sutter's former employee Heinrich Lienhard claimed that Sinclair left two hundred acres of fine ripe wheat standing unharvested when he took himself and his Indian crew off to prospect (a veiled criticism to illustrate Lienhard's views of gold fever-induced craziness) without mentioning that Sinclair was once more in charge of his normal affairs at home on April 18, or that he could supervise both locations without serious neglect of either, as his gold claim near modern Folsom was only a half-day's ride distant.[75] More than likely, though, John spent many nights away from home; and, though there is no further documentation, equally likely that the $16,000 Colonel Mason knew about in mid-July swelled to a larger sum.

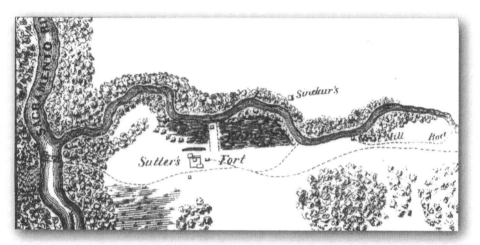

Lt. William T. Sherman drew this in 1848. Dotted lines from Sutter's Fort
to the American River indicate the location of the river crossing to reach the
Sinclair's Rancho del Paso. The mill race noted at far right is the site of Sutter's
water-powered gristmill. —Courtesy Sutter's Fort Museum Collection.

## Chapter 7

THE GOLD RUSH

By the time Mason began his tour of the gold fields in July, the gold frenzy had rapidly accelerated. When John first looked for gold in April, the relatively small influx of would-be prospectors hadn't unduly disrupted the pastoral tranquility of valley residents. But on May 12, enterprising merchant Sam Brannan rode through the streets of San Francisco, waving a bottle of gold specimens and shouting, "Gold on the American River!" Any disbelief still harbored in the minds of the majority evaporated immediately. Men abandoned their homes and businesses, sailors deserted their ships, and the only two newspapers in northern California suspended publication. The Gold Rush was on in earnest.

John Sinclair and his nearby Cosumnes River neighbors Jared Sheldon, William Daylor, Perry McCoon, and Martin Murphy Junior, hastened to the foothills with droves of cattle to sell to the miners as provisions-on-the-hoof. More gold rushers arrived every week from coastal towns and nearby valleys and—as trading ships spread the news—from Hawaii, Mexico, and South America. Word reached Monterey at the end of May, entirely disbelieved until Alcalde Walter Colton's hired man returned from the American River on June 20 with specimens, precipitating the predictable exodus of able-bodied men from that vicinity.[76]

Colonel Richard Mason, who had suffered some desertions in his own ranks at Monterey, yet had no official report of the fabulous gold finds he kept hearing about, determined to tour the gold districts himself. Accompanied by his adjutant Lieutenant William T. Sherman, Captain Joseph Folsom and a military escort, Mason rode through a nearly-deserted San Francisco, noted the vacant houses and idle mills along his route, and arrived at Sutter's Fort July 2, 1848. There he found more life and business: launches discharging their cargoes at the embarcadero and carts hauling goods to the several stores inside the complex. A two-story building inside the gates was being used as a hotel. Many people were camped outside the walls, some going and some coming, all swapping gold stories. Preparations were in progress to celebrate the Fourth of July—the first such occasion at the fort under the American Flag—and many more merrymakers, some coming from great distances, were expected to arrive shortly. Prevailed upon by Captain Sutter, who said he anticipated the presence of all the prominent men in the neighborhood, the colonel and his retinue agreed to stay for the festivities as Sutter's honored guests.

Samuel Kyburz, who ran the hotel inside the fort with his wife Rebecca, set up banquet tables in the old armory hall where, with the help of a number of women, he furnished an excellent meal for a private, gentlemen-only dinner. With a supply of good sauterne, brandy, and other alcoholic spirits on hand, said gentlemen drank freely. Charles "Philosopher" Pickett, a California resident since 1846, was the chosen "orator of the day" for the private gathering. Formerly a practicing lawyer and editor/publisher of the satirical *Flumgudgeon Gazette and Bumble Bee Budget* in Oregon City, Pickett was considered to be an entertaining eccentric by all who knew him. Instead, though, Sherman's memoir, *Recollections of California 1846-1861,* makes note of John Sinclair: "A man of some note, named Sinclair, presided, and after a substantial meal and a reasonable supply of *aguardiente* we began the toasts."

Impromptu speeches followed. Very soon, Sherman admitted, the participants were reduced to helpless fits of inebriated laughter.[77]

## A Lady in Distress

Mary Sinclair supplied another, quite different anecdotal tale of the July 4, 1848 celebration at Sutter's Fort.

Outside the banquet room, the assembled crowd was enjoying its own festivities with more patriotic speeches, dare-devil games and merriment. Mary was among them, chatting with the neighbors and probably helping with cooking. She was unburdened by motherhood responsibilities for a few hours, because she had left her nine-month-old daughter Amelia at home with an Indian girl servant.

Then the dancing began. The recent surge in the number of men in the area made the presence of women all the more relatively scarce, and it seemed to Mary that she continually whirled to the fiddler's lively tunes in the light of flaming bonfires. But as the moon's slender crescent rose she became more and more anxious, as would any young mother who had been away from her child longer than she had expected to be. Not wanting to spoil anyone else's fun, Mary forced herself to smile and laugh while the dancing continued without a break. Where was John? He was still at Captain Sutter's private party, and mid-nineteenth century wives didn't interrupt such gatherings merely with a plea to go home.

All at once a tall, slender young soldier appeared at her side. Speaking softly, he escorted her to a waiting team and wagon where, she was relieved to see, her husband was already aboard, though slumped in his seat from the effects of too much drink. The soldier sprang into the driver's seat and the trio drove rapidly over the dark, dusty road in the direction of the ranch, past groups of restless cattle. The screech owl's continuous din discouraged conversation, so it wasn't until Mary was safely home again that she learned the gallant young man's name: Lieutenant William T. Sherman.

Forty years later, Mary related this incident to her fellow New England Associated California Pioneers members in Boston. They, in turn, used her story as a delightful excuse to invite General William T. Sherman to join them as an honorary member. At a subsequent meeting the organization's president read aloud their letter to him, which included Mary's details, and General Sherman's reply. Their letter was printed in the *Boston Herald* but unfortunately the newspaper didn't include the answering correspondence from the General. He did, however, accept the society's invitation to become an honorary member.[78]

## A Touch of Madness

The numbers of men swarming into the gold fields multiplied daily, as did the proliferation of merchants who set up shops to mine the miners, and became rich from sales of mining tools and other merchandise. Colonel Mason's report estimated that approximately four thousand men were already engaged in mining when he toured the gold districts. Also, that the principal store at Sutter's Fort, Sam Brannan and Company, had received $36,000 in gold in payment for goods from the 1st of May to the 10th of July; and that other merchants had made extensive sales as well. Familiar faces reappeared, often with an entourage of new companions. Attorney and immigration promoter Lansford W. Hastings arrived with his fiancée, Charlotte Toler. Alcalde John Sinclair married the couple on July 19, 1848, at Sutter's Fort, as reported by the *Californian* on August 14.

At the beginning of the Gold Rush, when the focus was on Coloma and Mormon Island, Sinclair evidently suffered few depredations. Heinrich Lienhard, who kept a small flock of sheep east of John Sutter's trading post, remarked that several of his animals often disappeared at night. Whereas Sinclair, who, Lienhard said, owned about eighty head of sheep, had less exposure to the inroads of miners because the river cut Sinclair's ranch off from the main route to the mines.[79] That all changed, though, with the news of still more spectacular "strikes." A week after Major Pierson Reading dined with the Sinclairs in March 1848, he too visited Coloma. Afterward he returned to his rancho on the upper Sacramento River where, in six weeks, he mined $80,000 in gold from Clear Creek and adjacent present-day Trinity County. In June, the discovery of rich placers on the Feather River and its tributaries the Yuba and the Bear, sent fortune seekers arriving at the gravitational center of Sutter's Fort scurrying north over the well-known emigrant trail that skirted the Rancho del Paso. Better still, they just tromped directly through the property.

About August 16, 1848, yet another familiar person trundled into Sutter's Fort, driving oxcarts filled with saleable goods: young Moses Schallenberger of the 1844 Stephens-Murphy-Townsend Party, now an associate of Monterey merchant Thomas O. Larkin. He was a few days behind Charles Sterling, another Larkin associate, who had brought goods up from San Francisco to sell on the Yuba River at a hoped-for 300 to 500 percent profit. Both young men camped overnight near the Sinclairs residence, where they arranged to buy bullocks (young bulls) from John at $16 per animal, delivered in his corral. When castrated, these fetched $60-$70 per yoke, or pair, at the mining camps as working oxen. Yet if by August Sinclair's situation resembled Sutter's crumbling empire two miles west, or Theodore Cordua's similar adverse circumstances at his New Mecklenburg ranch near where gold had just been discovered on the Feather River, he likely had insufficient crew left to help drive the animals there. Or, he had simply decided that it was more prudent to stay on his ranch, which was rapidly becoming a little way-station to the diggings. Almost certainly he transacted other profitable business as a wholesale supplier, for retail prices had risen to unheard of heights. At the gold mines, beef-on-the-hoof cost sixty dollars, and horses sold for $100 to $150. These commodities were in abundance on the Rancho del Paso, which contained 16,000-18,000 cattle by the end of 1848. American wagons brought $300, and flour purchased at Sutter's Fort at $18 per 100 pounds resold for $30. Shoes were in great demand, as there were no inventories of this item to be found anywhere near the mining districts. Well-bred, principled Moses Schallenberger was shocked to discover that "self-interest is so great here that they can't take time to bury people when they die."

Gold had just been discovered on the upper Sacramento River, and at the head of the Cosumnes.[80]

News of the gold discovery had reached Oregon by ship in June, and as the fall season deepened the valley was further inundated by hordes caravanning from the north. Most of the newcomers, regardless of geographical origin, were peaceful, steady men who only wanted to find a fortune in the streams and gravels sufficient to indulge their dreams of a larger farm or lucrative business. But a seedier element, which congregated at the two new saloons and a billiard room that now occupied some of the deserted workshops inside Sutter's Fort, caused problems when excessive drink led to brawls and robbery. Yet another, more impudent faction thought nothing of poaching livestock, trampling through ripened grain fields, or helping themselves to unguarded foodstuffs and other articles. In combination, these reckless thugs were a nightmare for any civil magistrate.

The previous February Colonel Mason, charged with the duty of restoring and maintaining the peace, had made several alcalde appointments to prominent men throughout the territory, including his re-appointment of John Sinclair for the Sacramento District. It was a position John was reluctant to accept. Mason's answering correspondence (to John's letters) dated March 5, 1848, reads in part: "I sent to you but a few days since, upon the recommendation of Mr. Sutter, the appointment of alcalde, and am sorry to learn, by one of your letters...that you do not wish it. I am well aware of the difficulties that the alcalde has heretofore labored under. Those difficulties will soon be removed...I therefore hope you will not refuse the appointment, and that the public may have the benefit of your experience as an alcalde in putting the new machine in motion." [81]

In the end, John accepted Mason's appointment. Conditions in early March were so different from those that developed only three months hence when Mason, for all his good intentions, was unable to quash increasing troubles with squatters and general lawlessness. Perhaps coincident with notification that Mary's family was coming down from Oregon, John resigned his office sometime in September 1848, and that same month an election chose his successors. They were Franklin Bates, a brother of Dr. Henry Bates, as First Alcalde, and John S. Fowler as Second Alcalde. [82]

## Family Reunion

Mary's family, which consisted of her mother, seventeen-year-old sister Eliza, Eliza's husband William K. Beale, thirteen-year-old sister Amelia and brother Thomas Turner Eyre, aged nineteen, came by sea aboard the as-advertised "fast-sailing" brig *Henry*. Unhappily, the ship suffered an unspecified mishap that grounded it inside Baker's Bay even as other vessels skirted past it going out to sea. Eliza Eyre Beale—by then Mrs. Eliza Shepherd—shared the family's travel experience with a *Sacramento Union* reporter when she re-visited Sacramento in 1876, recalling that her family had suffered weeks of storms and discomforts aboard a stalled ship. Indeed, marine reports in Oregon and California newspapers confirm that the *Henry,* scheduled to leave Portland the week of September 10-17 loaded with flour, salmon, and 112 passengers, didn't succeed in getting out to sea until November 11. About a week later the family reached San Francisco, where they boarded a packet boat to New Helvetia. Which one, Eliza didn't say; C. L. Ross's fleet of small schooners *Ann, Caroline,* and *Wave* were among those available in the harbor for transport up the Sacramento River.[83] Upon reaching Sutter's embarcadero the weary family chanced to meet Captain Sutter and Major Pierson Reading who, with partner Samuel Hensley, maintained a mercantile at the fort; and Captain William Warner of the Army's Topographical Engineers. All three gentlemen, Eliza claimed, graciously escorted them to the Rancho del Paso.

If the image of the Sinclair's ranch house exterior is hazy, this time we can follow someone inside. Eliza described her sister's residence as "a fine home...with every comfort."[84] Coming from a feminine perspective, this praise indicates that the house was appointed with glass windows, curtains, and scattered carpets; well-crafted tables, seating, and storage cabinets, perhaps a cushioned armchair or two. "Every comfort" would include generous amounts of tableware and cookware, and comfortable bedding and pillows. The pantry was sure to contain flour and home-canned vegetables. The pastured livestock promised future meals of beef, pork, and lamb. Chickens roaming about the yard provided eggs, and fowl for the stewpot; there were milch cows for milk and butter and cheese.

These domestic attributes were doubtless most appreciated by Mary's mother who was not only large with child, but also the defendant in an acrimonious divorce and custody suit filed in Oregon by her second husband, James C. Campbell. Since Campbell's suit dated in August 1848 sought custody of the couple's year-old daughter Susannah and their unborn child, Mrs. Campbell's delivery date was likely close at hand when the family arrived. Eyre family researchers believe that John Campbell, who lived to adulthood, was born in California in early 1849. Susannah remained in Oregon, with her father.

It was already late in that first Gold Rush mining season, but the fabled California climate held to its normal winter rainy season with extended periods of pleasant dry weather. According to Eliza Beale Shepherd, an excited William Beale took Thomas Eyre with him to the North Fork of the American River where the pair formed a company, with twenty-eight others, to turn the river at a spot which became known as Beale's Bar. This was very near Sinclair's earlier claim, so John must have guided them there, and probably continued his own mining efforts, while the ladies remained at the ranch. The mining company was successful. Beale's Bar developed into a community that was still active in 1855.[85]

*Chapter 8*

NEW DEVELOPMENTS

News of the gold discovery had only reached the western frontier of the United States at St. Louis in August, and therefore the ships which had left the East Coast in the spring to round the Horn as yet carried no gold-seekers. On September 14, 1848, the *Huntress*, 150 days out of New York, arrived at San Francisco with a passenger who had sailed all the way from Switzerland—Captain John Sutter's eldest son, Johann August Sutter, Junior. August, as he was addressed, a young man still five weeks shy of his twenty-second birthday, was beset with rumors of his father's imminent ruin almost as soon as he stepped off the gangplank. Upon reaching the fort, August spent several days studying his father's ledgers, his alarm growing with each page he turned. Sutter senior, too, was growing more harried. His many creditors, who now erroneously assumed he was rich, were swooping in to collect their past due payments.

At the urging of his "advisors," Captain Sutter transferred title of his real estate to August on October 14, a tactic employed in the hope of forestalling clamoring creditors. Then he left for the mountains again, hoping to find the rich gold-field that had so far eluded him.

August was left on his own at the fort, amidst utter chaos. Earnest and conscientious, and desperate to settle his father's accounts so that the Sutter family might retain at least a portion of the New Helvetia land

grant, August was easily manipulated by Sam Brannan and other prominent men. A number of merchants wanted to build shops on the water-
front—the better to snare gold miners as they debarked from upriver
boats—even though most of them already had shops two miles east of
the Sacramento River, at Sutter's Fort. They assured August that if he
would establish a town, the sale of lots would raise immediate and substantial funds with which to repay his father's debts. Well-meaning, and
seeing no other way to accomplish his objectives, August acquiesced. He
hired Army captain William H. Warner to do the surveying and mapping.
With the aid of lieutenants William T. Sherman and Edward O. C. Ord,
Warner completed his task in late December 1848.

In the same month another new arrival, fresh from the mines on
the Yuba River, passed through Sutter's Fort en route to San Francisco.
This was Peter Hardeman Burnett, the former captain of Mary Sinclair's
Oregon-bound wagon train back in 1843. In the intervening years, Burnett
had risen to Judge of the Oregon territorial supreme court. August hired
Peter Burnett as his lawyer and business manager, and in early January
Burnett presided at the auction for the sale of city lots. When John Sutter
at last returned from the mountains he was furious, but it was too late.
The city of Sacramento was born, a major, and perhaps unsettling, trans-
formation of the relaxed country environment that the Sinclairs had lived
in for so long.[86]

Although he was no longer the alcalde, John Sinclair remained a re-
spected and involved member of his community as the new city on the
riverfront rapidly expanded. A multitude of tents, and some hastily constructed shanties, materialized on the levee. Hensley, Reading & Company
removed from the fort to build the first frame structure at the corner of
Front and I Streets. Barton Lee and his partner Albert Priest, who had
been Mary's family's fellow passengers on the *Henry* with their small stock
of gum boots and coarse blankets, soon followed with a frame-and-canvas
store at 2nd and J Streets.[87] But those firms and several others that had
rented or purchased storefront space at the fort were still doing business
there in late 1848 when a dispute over territorial rights ended in a killing.

Charles E. Pickett, the same man who had been orator of the day at Sutter's July Fourth dinner, was by now renting space in the fort's northwest bastion and its adjoining ground, where he operated a general store. Pickett's lease agreement also included a storage room south of, and adjacent to, the bastion, which had a connecting door. Isaac Alderman, lately from Oregon, claimed that Sutter had leased *him* the storage room. Reportedly, this dispute had twice been decided in Pickett's favor by the alcalde—probably Second Alcalde John Fowler, since First Alcalde Franklin Bates was, according to some accounts, a business partner of Alderman's. Nonetheless, adversarial opinions between the two contenders grew heated. Pickett forbade Alderman to use the connecting door into the storage room.

Alderman was known as a violent and unprincipled man. Charles Pickett was generally affable but proved to be tougher than Alderman supposed. After uselessly warning Alderman off, Pickett nailed the connecting door shut—whereupon Alderman advanced on him, brandishing an ax. Pickett, forced to retreat backwards until his back was against a wall, grabbed up his shotgun and fired. Alderman fell over dead. This altercation occurred December 6, 1848, towards nighttime. Alcalde Bates refused to act, instead delegating authority to his second, John Fowler, who resigned two days later. Public opinion was mixed, yet most felt it was a case of justifiable homicide until merchant Sam Brannan claimed it was murder, and demanded a trial.

On the evening of December 9, a somewhat unorthodox trial commenced at the fort, in a room soon overflowing with witnesses and spectators. Sam Brannan, who had been elected that afternoon to act as judge for the trial, appointed himself the prosecuting attorney as well. According to one observer, the solemnity of the proceedings disintegrated in a haze of cigar smoke and watered brandy consumed by the participants—including the defendant. Hours dragged by, until it was past midnight. Jury foreman John Sinclair and juror John Sutter, each enveloped in a Mexican *serape,* their chairs tipped back against a wall, fell fast asleep during a portion of the testimony. When the jury was unable to unanimously agree on a verdict, Pickett was released on a $10,000 bond provided by Sam Brannan and John Sinclair. A second trial produced the same result, with Brannan and Sinclair still acting as bondsmen. "Philosopher" Pickett was exonerated at his third trial, which probably ended mid-December. Someone traveling downriver to San Francisco told the editors of the *California Star & Californian*; they printed "Acquittal of C.E. Pickett" on December 23.[88]

According to Sam Brannan's clerk William Grimshaw, who was a juror at Pickett's third trial, the Pickett-Alderman incident was the impetus that prompted a number of responsible citizens in Sacramento to consider forming a provisional government, which would include mechanisms for adjudicating future felonious acts. The more serious concern, though, was the lack of any governmental oversight at all. Headed by Peter Burnett, who was sworn in as California's first elected civil governor by year's end, several men met on January 6, and again on January 8, 1849. They were aware that other groups in San Francisco and San Jose were debating the very same issue, after learning that Congress had adjourned without making provision for a government in California. All present at the Sacramento meetings agreed that their actions were necessary because the gold discovery "...had attracted and would continue to attract an immense migration from all parts of the world, adding to a precarious state of affairs, a present state of confusion and temptation to crime... [and] whereas Congress had so far failed to formally extend the laws of the United States to California Territory."

A sub-committee consisting of Sam Brannan, John Sinclair, Pierson Reading, John Fowler and Barton Lee were assigned the task of preparing suitable documents. The second meeting closed with the recommendation that the Sacramento District should elect five delegates to attend a provisional government convention scheduled for March 5, 1849, in San Jose. On January 10, the election of delegates resulted in the unanimous choice of John A. Sutter, John Sinclair, Samuel Brannan, M.D. Winship, and Samuel Hensley. On February 11, 1849, John Sinclair wrote to the San Francisco committee objecting to a proposed postponement of the

convention until May 1. One of the original five elected delegates must
have withdrawn and been replaced with an alternate, because he signed
this letter with "John Sinclair [and] C. E. Pickett, Members of [the]
Convention Elect." [89]

That letter to the San Francisco committee, published in the *Alta
California* on March 1, 1849, is the last time Sinclair's name appears in
print in association with events in California. If at first John and Mary
intended to assimilate into the new and exciting social and political fab-
ric, accumulating negative factors had to be weighed as well. John's
business mentor, partner and friend of many years Eliab Grimes, a man
with vast experience in seafaring and mercantile activities, and whose
integrity and alliances with other traders and officials of many nations
were renowned, had died in San Francisco on November 7, 1848. Eliab's
death legally dissolved the partnership. His will bequeathed his majority share in the Rancho del Paso to his nephew Hiram Grimes, until
then a partner with little personal involvement in the daily management
of the property. More pertinent, undoubtedly, were the rapid changes
engulfing the "old time" California pioneers. If later warnings published
by Hiram Grimes, John Sutter and other landowners are indications of
the problems the Sinclairs experienced, then disruptive squatters, tree-
choppers, horse thieves, and wanton livestock butcheries caused frequent distress. Even those who were peaceable stopped by all too often
as "guests" to impose on the traditional hospitality offered to travelers
by all Californians.

Rumors, and guesstimates from San Francisco Harbor officials,
warned that hundreds, if not thousands, were aboard ships on their way
to flood the region with even more manic gold-seekers, and everyone
knew another overland travel season would begin in the spring. Whether
it was one frightening incident or a collection of unpleasant experiences,
John and Mary felt endangered. They decided to relocate to the far less
tumultuous East Coast. [90]

Sketch of Sacramento City as it looked in late 1849, five months after the Sinclairs sailed for the East. —Author's collection.

*Chapter 9*

LEAVING

On February 27, 1849, just sixteen days after John's written objection to a change of date for the provisional government convention, he and Mary deeded their interests in the Rancho del Paso, and the adjoining Rancho San Juan, to Hiram Grimes for $5,000. This document was signed in the presence of Sacramento's First Magistrate Henry Schoolcraft on March 29, 1849.[91]

Sutter's Fort Archives has a short letter from John Sinclair to James Reed dated April 5, 1848, headed "Rancho del Paso" and clearly penned by a hurried man with much on his mind. "I expect to leave here on Monday next on [our] way to the U. S. and not knowing whether I would have time to write you from San Francisco or not I send you a few lines from here," John wrote, further informing Reed that "Captain J. B. Chiles is in charge of the farm." However, in April 1848, Joseph Ballinger Chiles was in Missouri organizing another emigrant wagon train and did not re-enter California until October. It looks as if, in his haste, John wrote 1848 instead of 1849, and the family therefore departed on Monday, April 10, 1849, to sail downriver to San Francisco Bay. Mary's sister Eliza didn't accompany them. According to her own account, Eliza Eyre Beale joined her husband William at Beale's Bar, and came back with him in the winter of 1849 to learn that Hiram Grimes had sold the Rancho del Paso to Samuel Norris. [92] After exploring opportunities in Sacramento city, the couple returned to Oregon the following July. The U. S.-bound travelers in April consisted of the Sinclairs and their toddler-aged daughter Amelia, Mary's mother Eliza Campbell and her infant son John Campbell, Mary's sister Amelia, and two unidentified servants.

Several months earlier, the Pacific Mail steamship *California* had sailed from New York on its maiden voyage, to inaugurate U. S. mail service between Panama and San Francisco. The ship departed on October 6, 1848, headed for the Straits of Magellan.

Therefore, the crew and passengers were unaware of the wild gold excitement generated when President Polk's State of the Union address to Congress on December 5, 1848, confirmed circulating rumors that gold in California was indeed abundant and rich. When the ship reached Panama City in mid-January 1849, ailing Captain Cleveland Forbes was confronted with hundreds of frenzied gold-seekers who had crossed the Isthmus and now demanded to board his vessel. Feeling too ill to continue his duties, Forbes relinquished his command to Captain John Marshall, who had boarded the ship at Valparaiso. Bursting with would-be gold miners, the *California* entered the Golden Gate on February 28, 1849, and anchored in the Bay—whereupon her entire crew deserted for the gold fields, including Captain Marshall.

When the Sinclairs arrived from their ranch no fewer than thirty-eight vessels stranded by deserting crews clogged the harbor at San Francisco, but on April 18 the *California* was the only vessel at anchor destined for Panama and intermediate ports. Ever conscientious despite his ill health, Cleveland Forbes had arranged for the *California's* safety in port, and agreed to resume command for the return voyage to Panama. Advertisements in the *Weekly Alta California* announced that the ship would sail in mid-April, yet it was April 29 before Captain Forbes, obliged for the first time in his career to coax sailors with hat in hand and exorbitant wages, had gathered sufficient crew. On April 26, 1849, the *Alta* erroneously reported that the *California* was to depart that day and published a list of outbound passengers, most of them with first names omitted. John and Mary Sinclair were not on this list, an inexplicable oversight since "Campbell, daughter and servant"—Mary's mother Eliza Campbell and her sister Amelia—are. Other passengers named in the *Alta* were Mrs. Grimes and son, the family of John Sinclair's former partner Hiram Grimes, who had relocated from Hawaii to San Francisco in 1847. Mrs. Frances Smith was returning home after accompanying her husband, General Persifor Frazer Smith, on his trip west. Smith had come to California to split, between himself and General Bennet Riley, Colonel Richard Mason's dual duties as military governor and commander of the Army's Department of the Pacific. Also listed was Jane (Mrs. John) McDougal, one of the ship's thirty-five cabin passengers, who kept a journal of her voyage to Panama and beyond.

Priced at $250, the *California*'s stateroom cabins represented first-class accommodations. Each contained three berths, one above another, together with a cushioned locker which could accommodate another passenger. Each stateroom had a mirror, a toilet stand, washbowl, water bottle and drinking glasses. Still, they were just rooms, not suites. It seems reasonable to assume that John Sinclair booked one for his family and another for his in-laws.

The *California* at last set sail from San Francisco on Tuesday, May 1. The following day Colonel Richard Mason, who had relinquished his military governorship to General Bennet Riley in April, boarded the ship when it made its scheduled stop at Monterey. Mrs. McDougal's journal names Mason and several other fellow passengers (only a few of whom can be identified for certain since she didn't record first names), and their activities aboard ship, including the fact that most of them were seasick for the first few days, a condition they remedied with brandy and water.

It is this journal that confirms John and Mary Sinclair's passage on the *California* although Jane appears not to have developed a close friendship with the couple, misspells their name as St. Claire, and never makes note of meeting Eliza Campbell or any other family member. Colonel Mason, it will be remembered, had corresponded with John Sinclair regarding the official duties of alcaldes. The two had met in person at Sutter's Fort in July 1848, and Mason had included a sample from John's gold claim with his official report to Washington, D.C. Nothing tells us whether the two men formed a new, more informal bond on the journey, but surely both were among the other male passengers who helped Captain Forbes quash a threatened mutiny in mid-May while the ship was in Mexican waters. On May 5, Jane McDougal paid a social call on the Sinclairs and Mrs. Grimes. On May 22 she noted that "Mr. St. Claire," Mrs. Grimes, and others played whist all evening.

After the ship made port at Panama in the late afternoon of May 23, Jane McDougal and other ladies, including Mrs. Grimes, took rooms at the American Hotel to await the finalization of arrangements to cross the Isthmus. Jane last mentions the Sinclairs on Sunday May 27, when Sinclair breakfasted with her and her companions, and then spent the day shopping in Panama, returning with his wife at dinnertime to dine with Jane and her party. The next day Jane set off for the trek across the Isthmus. Presumably the Sinclair family did likewise, but with a different group. From May 28 forward, Jane speaks only of her own circle of friends.

The land trip across the fifty-mile wide Isthmus had its risks: invisible, virulent diseases such as cholera, yellow fever and malaria lurked everywhere to infect travelers who were exposed to the elements throughout the journey. The mountainous section from Panama City to either Gongora or Cruces (considered the better route) astride mules, took an entire twelve hours and usually cost from twelve to fifteen dollars per person. Baggage was transported at $44 per 180 pounds. At the end of the rough and muddy mule path, another dangerous adventure awaited:

transport down the Chagres River by dug-out canoes known as "bungo boats," poled by natives through steaming jungles. Jane McDougal arrived in Chagres on May 29, worn but healthy, and sailed away the next day on an English ship bound for Philadelphia. The other groups of travelers might have reached the Atlantic side about the same time, even though Mrs. McDougal and her friends had taken a whaleboat downriver from Cruces, not a bungo.[93] Tired and dirty, everyone was eager to leave Panama behind.

But John Sinclair, and little twenty-month-old Amelia, had contracted a deadly illness.

**Devastation**

At Chagres, as the New Orleans *Picayune* reported, "Mr. Sinclair, three ladies and two servants" boarded the steamship *Crescent City* bound for New Orleans and New York. Colonel Richard Mason was on the same ship, scheduled to disembark at New Orleans for the next leg of his journey to an assigned military post in St. Louis. On June 11 the *New Orleans Bee* reported that the vessel, commanded by veteran shipmaster Captain Charles Stoddard, had arrived at the Port of New Orleans on Sunday June 10 after a notably fast voyage, having left Chagres on June 4—without adding that John Sinclair died onboard June 10, 1849, as the *Crescent City* was entering the harbor.

Other newspapers picked up the story, almost certainly because someone let it be known to the press that this otherwise ordinary person was the man who had been involved with the nationally-famous Donner Party rescue two years earlier. The *Daily Picayune*'s somewhat florid prose claimed that John had been ambulatory enough to see and appreciate the sights of the harbor before expiring.

Proper medical attention had stopped his symptoms, the Washington, D.C., *Daily Union* wrote, but "his violent diarrhea was brought on again by imprudent eating and drinking. He made his will, giving $10,000 dollars to his brother and sister, and leaving the rest to his wife and child. [His] child...died also at New Orleans the day after the *Crescent City*'s arrival." The Baltimore *Sun* reported that the deceased child was a young daughter. A half-century later, editors compiling *The History of Lexington* erroneously stated that the child who had died at New Orleans had been an infant son.

One newspaper frankly stated cholera as the cause of death; others substituted the oft-used euphemism diarrhea, which covered a range of ailments. Newspaper reports of the amount of gold John Sinclair was carrying ranged from $30,000 to $80,000 to $100,000. On June 27 the *Daily Union* printed this: "We have been requested to state that the relatives of Mr. John Sinclair will hear of something to their advantage by calling at the office of Joseph Hoxie, Esq., in Wall Street." All eastern newspaper articles said he was thirty-nine and was either a native or former resident of Brooklyn, New York. None mentioned Scotland as his birthplace.[94]

John had been a Mexican citizen since 1841. Now, he was entitled to declare himself an American under the terms of Colonel Richard Mason's Proclamation to the People of Upper California, dated at Monterey August 7, 1848, and published in the *Californian* September 2, 1848. Upon receiving official confirmation that the treaty ending the war with Mexico had been ratified by both nations, Mason gave all Mexican citizens of California automatic American citizenship unless they decided otherwise within one year. John's last will and testament dated June 10, 1849, is only a few sentences:

*I John Sinclair a citizen of the United States and late resident of California being now of sound mind do hereby solemnly swear this to be my last Will and Testament to wit: I do hereby give and bequeath the sum of ten thousand dollars out of any monies or effects belonging to my estate real or personal unto my brothers and sisters to be divided and shared equally between them. The remainder of all my estate real or personal of whatsoever nature or kind so ever I do hereby give and bequeath unto my wife Mary Sinclair for her sole use and benefit. In testimony whereof I have hereunto subscribed my name and set my seal on board the Steam Ship Crescent City this tenth day of June in the year of our Lord one thousand eight hundred and forty nine.*

The will was witnessed by Josiah Hopper, M.D., John Rudenstier, M.D., U.S.N.—the physicians who attended him aboard the *Crescent City*—and fellow passenger Lewis H. Thomas, a native of Liverpool, England. All of them attested to having had a short acquaintance with the deceased. Obviously, one or more of these witnesses leaked the contents of the will to reporters, and no doubt contributed to the confusion over the amount of gold the Sinclairs were carrying.

It is Mary's petition for probate dated at New York on June 26, 1849, which supplies more detail. She gives the names of John's brothers Hugh and Cameron Sinclair, and his sisters Isabella and Jane Sinclair, all of whom "severally resided in the city of New York." The petition further states that "the widow, heirs and next of kin...are your petitioner Mary Sinclair, the widow of John Sinclair...and Amelia Sinclair the only child of said deceased who departed this life in a few hours after the death of the said testator...who was only twenty months of age...that said deceased left no other child or children or descendants of any deceased child or children than the above named Amelia Sinclair him surviving, nor any parent and no other heirs and next of kin than the above named brothers and sisters." [95]

There are no death certificates in New Orleans for either father or child, but there is a valid reason these are not on file. Louisiana did not legally require the registration of deaths occurring inside its borders until 1918, and even then it was still, as it had been for generations, solely the family's responsibility to appear at the Parish Clerk's Office to record the death. Mary Sinclair, a non-resident, was either ignorant of this custom, too grief-stricken to make the effort, or unable to go there in person because of the catastrophe New Orleans itself was experiencing. Five weeks before the *Crescent City* entered the harbor, the Mississippi River had breached the levy at a sugarcane plantation owned by Pierre Sauvé, some fifteen miles above the city. Torrents of water thundered in, widening the gap as it destroyed everything in its path. By early June, the floodwaters had swirled into urbanized areas to inundate 220 city blocks. The flood, known as Sauvé's Crevasse, displaced thousands from their homes. On the days that John and Amelia died, water was still standing in several city streets and others were obstructed by alluvion deposits of decaying animal and vegetable matter. Still, according to the Williams Research Center in New Orleans, those conditions should not have interfered with burials, or with long-established systems to record them.[96]

The Archdiocese of New Orleans reported that John and Amelia were not laid to rest in any Catholic cemetery, and suggested that they were probably quickly buried in a public graveyard. Nonetheless, a personal search through the New Orleans city-owned cemetery archives comes up empty. This search includes Charity Hospital, an agency whose duty it was to bury the city's resident poor, as well as newly-arrived transient persons, in their own graveyard on high ground on the outskirts of town. If Sinclair is not buried in New Orleans, then Mary might have taken the remains of her husband and daughter on with her for interment in New York—in a family plot on private land—because no New York City cemetery founded in or before June 1849 has a record of their burial. At this time cremation was forbidden in New Orleans, but other methods of preparing the dead for transport were commonly employed, and the Sinclairs had money in their luggage. The practice of transporting human bodies in ship hulls was hardly unheard of, despite the fact that it often made other passengers superstitiously uncomfortable. Possibly the remains were packed in salts or strongly-scented soap, as embalming wasn't widely available until the Civil War era. And maybe the bodies were consigned to the sea once the ship resumed its journey northward. Bereaved families strongly resisted this if they had any choice in the matter, because a watery grave denied them the established tradition of a concrete final resting place, and a lasting memorial to a life lived, where they might go to grieve.

⊣⊢⊨

The *Crescent City* sailed from New Orleans on June 16 via Havana and made port at New York on Saturday, June 23, with up to a million dollars in gold in her hold. Of this, $490,514 was freight consigned to specific individuals or companies. The amount listed to consignee John Sinclair was $30,000—although *The Spectator* took care to inform its readers that amounts brought by passengers in personal luggage had not yet been ascertained. Another probate document Mary signed in New York on July 2 stated that the value of the property of the deceased consisted of gold dust invoiced at $30,000, but when smelted might turn out to be only about $25,000.[97]

Word of John Sinclair's death didn't reach California until August, at which time the press misinformed its readers and future historians by repeating one eastern paper's "died yesterday morning" statement instead of printing the actual June date provided in another publication. San Francisco and Sacramento newspapers did broaden the information they received to include a generalized homage to Sinclair's status and accomplishments in California, noting his "numerous circle of friends." Yet those editors, who undeniably counted many pioneers among their contacts, declined to print any specific details they may have gathered locally, and also neglected to mention John's wife or daughter. Respectful regret for an esteemed man who had died took second place behind the more exciting focus of their attention: the ever-intensifying fever of the California Gold Rush.[98]

Much remains a mystery about John Sinclair. We don't know his date of birth; only that, had he lived, he would have celebrated a fortieth birthday by the end of 1849. His parents' names are unknown, and there were sixty boys named John Sinclair born or baptized in Scotland during the years 1808-1811. His few extant writings confirm that he had complete command of both formal and vernacular English, but we don't know where he received his fine education. A standard practice at the "better" schools was to have young students memorize long tracts of revered writings. Since John so readily quoted lines from Lord Byron's poetry which were eerily relevant to the Donner Party tragedy in his 1847 letter to Alcalde Bartlett, it is tempting to speculate that he spent his boyhood years at Scotland's centuries-old, prestigious Aberdeen Academy, Byron's own alma mater.

Unfortunately, Aberdeen suffered a twentieth century fire that destroyed most of its nineteenth century student records. John's advanced schooling, if any, might have been acquired at any British or American college.

We don't know when he came to America. Dozens of men named Sinclair emigrated to the United States in the 1810s, 1820s and early 1830s, yet a search of immigration records found no matches with John's known siblings. The Hudson's Bay Company did, in fact, employ someone named John Sinclair for some years in Oregon, but that man was a blacksmith, a skill never attributed, by any source, to John Sinclair of Rancho del Paso. We have no physical description of him, supporting the notion that his appearance was ordinary: not too tall or too short, neither handsome nor ugly; not a redhead. Doubtless his body was toned and muscular, hardly unusual for a rancher/farmer of any decade. In John's time and place, the style for men's facial hair included a mustache and longish sideburns. No one ever commented whether he wore this look, or was clean-shaven.

We don't know where he is buried. In some respects, he remains ethereal.

A sketch of Mary Sinclair Davis, published in *Kansas City Journal* February 6, 1898. —Author's collection.

*Chapter 10*

## RELIVING THE GOLDEN DAYS OF OLD

Mary Sinclair lived on for another sixty years. We can only imagine her anguish and emotional turmoil in June 1849. She had suddenly lost both her husband and her only child, all the more devastating because it happened in a strange city so far from home. Doubtless the distraught widow received aid from the *Crescent City*'s master Captain Stoddard. We might also assume she received comfort and advice from the two doctors on the ship who witnessed John's will, one of whom resided in New York. Mary, her mother Eliza and her sister Amelia were aboard the *Crescent City* when it sailed from New Orleans on June 16 to continue their journey east, where longer-term support was waiting in New England in the person of Captain William Dane Phelps.

Mary Sinclair had a connection with William Phelps, one created years before by two men who found compatible qualities in each other. Recall that during the years 1840-1842, Captain Phelps was engaged in the California hide and tallow trade as master of the ship *Alert*. In July 1841, he cruised up the Sacramento River in a smaller craft to visit John Sutter, and met John Sinclair. Captain Phelps spent an enjoyable week exploring and elk-hunting with Sutter and then-bachelor Sinclair, establishing an even closer friendship with John when the two departed in Phelps's boat to sail downriver on a five-day trip to San Francisco Bay. There, Phelps rejoined the *Alert* and Sinclair boarded the *Lama* for a brief sojourn in Hawaii. In April 1842, Phelps again came upriver to visit Captain Sutter, and again re-connected with John Sinclair. Given their friendship, and the fact that letters were the primary, and customary, means of communication in the pioneer era, it is reasonable to suppose the two stayed in contact through correspondence after Phelps sailed for his Massachusetts home in December 1842.

Three years passed. Captain Phelps revisited California waters in September 1845 as master of the bark *Moscow*, sailing from port to port until his trading activities were interrupted the following year by the Mexican-American War. One wartime adventure after another, and the subsequent resumption of normal business, kept him on the Pacific Coast through and beyond the gold discovery. He went to the mines twice in the summer of 1848, affording him ample time and proximity to pay a visit to John Sinclair, and meet John's wife Mary. As Phelps was a thoughtful and courteous man, we might assume that he invited the couple to be his guests should they ever be in Boston. Captain William Dane Phelps departed California in October 1848 as a ship's passenger, and arrived home in Lexington, Massachusetts, in February 1849, four months before John's death at New Orleans.[99]

Whether Captain Phelps initially learned of Mary's personal tragedy by direct correspondence from Mary herself, or from other sources, is unknown. It is quite probable that John Sinclair shared the opinion of a mutual friend, Thomas Larkin, who told his wife during the Mexican-American War that if anything happened to him she should turn to Captain Phelps, saying, "You will look on him as a good and honest man as there is in this country." Whatever the method of communication—or the reason behind it—that prompted contact between William Phelps and Mary in 1849, he did in fact offer her his personal protection at his Boston-suburb residence. He welcomed her into his home and family, which consisted of his wife Lusanna and two pre-adolescent daughters. He, too, had recently suffered a wrenching loss, the death of his four-year-old son. The Phelps family, and Mary Sinclair, are recorded at this household on the census dated August 30, 1850—but the startling entry is for one Ann Sinclair, aged nine, born in California.[100]

She cannot be John's daughter with his Hawaiian first wife. That child would be eleven in 1850, not nine, and anyway was almost certainly born in Hawaii before John departed for California. Mary Sinclair's testimony in her June 1849 petition for probate emphatically stated that John had no child other than Amelia, a twenty-month-old girl who outlived him by only a few hours. Clearly, the five-year-old daughter of whom John was so proud back in 1844 died at some point during his marriage to Mary, a personal loss that was all too common considering the nineteenth century's 20-30 percent child mortality statistics. Ann Sinclair—who herself disappears from the official record after 1850—must be a niece who happened to be visiting when the census taker came to the Phelps residence.

Nineteenth century census takers made many mistakes as they went door to door collecting data. Yet, since we have so few personal details of John's life, there is no reason to discount the veracity of Ann's birthplace. It appears, then, that in 1841 one of John's brothers came to California with a pregnant wife. The question of exactly when, that year, cannot be answered. Captain Phelps, whose voluminous journal entries noted many things, didn't record the presence of family during his visit in late July-early August. John himself was in Hawaii, or traveling to and from, from August 8 to November 11. If nothing else, Ann's California birth and her later presence in the Phelps household, when combined with Sinclair's generous bequest to his brothers and sisters, indicates that John and his siblings enjoyed a close relationship despite the distances that separated them. Even more, it shows that at least one brother and sister-in-law made the effort to affirm that bond in person, and later developed affectionate ties with his widow.

## Predicament in Oregon

Mary Sinclair lived with the Phelps family until she remarried in 1852, but her own relatives weren't there to help celebrate the wedding. In the spring of 1850 her mother, half-brother John Campbell, and her sister

Amelia had again crossed the plains to Oregon, this time with Mary's brother Thomas. Thomas Eyre had returned to Oregon sometime in 1849, where he used his mined gold to purchase a farm. There, he must have received a letter from Mary via a Pacific Mail steamer, imploring him to come east to escort their female relatives back home. This he did, at more cost to himself than he anticipated.

In March 1851, Mary Sinclair wrote to her late husband's long-time friend Thomas O. Larkin, asking him to facilitate a transfer of $2,400 she wished to send to her brother. Stiff and formal, the short letter was probably dictated as she wrote by someone who understood the intricacies of the banking system; in particular, the inability of Boston banks to transact business with their Oregon counterparts. "I am desirous of remitting to Oregon a sum of money to meet the wants of my brother and family, who having arrived at Salem...and being short of funds owing to unforeseen circumstances have written to me for assistance," she began. The favor she asked was for Larkin to forward the sum from his own bank in California and collect from Mary's Boston account with added commission and expenses.

Enclosed with her letter to Thomas Larkin was another written by Captain William Dane Phelps, who addressed Larkin familiarly as *Don Tomas:*

> *Mrs. Sinclair received letters by the last mail from Oregon from her brother stating that they had safely arrived, but his detention and losses on the road had reduced his funds...and worse than all, on his arrival found that the friend in whose charge he had left his farm and also his papers relating to it had sold the property at a very low price. This was a sad disappointment as he had his mother and sister with him, and expecting to have a house and home of his own to have taken them to...He is a very deserving and industrious young man ... He writes that he has contracted for another farm and was preparing to cultivate it, but was lacking $2,400 to pay for it...Mrs. Sinclair will assist to the amount, and I thought the safest and best way to get the funds to him would be to request you to arrange it for them.*

Phelps went on to say that Mary would not let her "only and dear brother suffer if she could prevent it," then added a parental-like plea: "If you see Mr. Eyre...would you ascertain from him what his situation actually is. He is not very prone to write particulars... anything you can do for him by advice or otherwise will be highly appreciated by Mrs. Sinclair." He closed with a description of Thomas (slender, small-statured, reddish hair), and personal amenities. "Nothing of interest has transpired since you left here (Boston and New York)...Please remember me to old "amigos." [101]

## New Life, Old Ties

On November 25, 1852, Mary married Sidney Glass Davis, a Lexington resident who was about her same age. Sidney worked for Bigelow & Davis, a company located on North Market Street in Boston, which advertised itself as "Produce Commission Merchants for the Sale of Flour, Butter, Cheese and Western Produce Generally." The firm's owners were T. B. Bigelow, C. O. Davis, and John Davis. As near as can be affirmed, Sidney G. Davis was not a principle in this business until the late 1850s-early 1860s.

Over a period of fourteen years Mary and Sidney had six children: Ada, Walter, Clara, Allan, Marion, and Fanny. Ada, the firstborn, died in 1859 at age six. Sidney and Mary Sinclair Davis—she kept the Sinclair identity as part of her name for the rest of her life—were married for forty years, until his death on December 31, 1892. [102]

In the meantime, over the years scores of former California gold-rushers had returned to their eastern homes, with or without a fortune, to their anxiously waiting families. Most of them cherished lustrous memories of their participation in the heady, chaotic, fantastic California Gold Rush. By and by, throughout the eastern states, these men formed fraternal organizations which met annually (or more often), where they shared their memories and experiences in private-home parlors or public venues. Over time they admitted their own wives as auxiliary members, and eventually welcomed the membership of other women who had themselves been in California during the golden days of old.

One of these groups, in Boston, was the New England Associated California Pioneers of '49, also known as the Associated Forty-Niners of Boston, who proudly considered Mary Sinclair Davis as one of their valued members. At the association's first annual grand reunion reception at Boston's Revere House in March 1890, Mary was seated next to its president Samuel Snow, while he and others traded tales of their harrowing journeys to the gold fields by sea around Cape Horn, or across the Isthmus of Panama's dense jungles, or overland in covered wagons. (The Boston *Herald* opined that some of their reminiscences sounded more like the tales of the *Arabian Nights,* than of actual experiences.)[103]

In November 1890, as Sutter's Fort in far-away but long-remembered California was in process of its first restoration, this association sent a check to the Sacramento Society of California Pioneers for $100, a consolidation of separate donations to the cause from "genuine Forty-niners." Most of the individual donations—from "men of old who dug for gold too poor nowadays to carry out the wishes of their hearts," as association secretary George G. Spurr stated in his cover letter—were less than five dollars. Mary Sinclair Davis donated two dollars. In 1893, at their fifty-seventh monthly meeting, the association's board of directors voted Mary in as a life member. She remained active in the New England Associated California Pioneers, serving yearly on the Ladies' Committee on Reception, through 1898.

The organization's 1893 reunion and banquet was jovially described as a "veritable old-fashioned miners' meeting" lasting eight hours.[104] The 1898 reunion—the fiftieth anniversary of the gold discovery—was by far the most exciting of all, despite nearly every member having passed the age of seventy. Mary Sinclair Davis was again honored at this celebration, where she recounted a story to a news reporter of having seen and handled the first gold specimens that James Marshall took from the tailrace of Sutter's sawmill. Mary is quoted as saying that the day Marshall came to tell Captain Sutter his exciting news, he stopped en route to show the Sinclairs his new-found treasure, because the road from the mill site to Sutter's Fort took him past their home. Only Mary and the newsman know what she actually said. Perhaps the reporter was pushing his elderly subject for sensational copy on this hallowed, yet "old news" occasion, because the assertion as printed is that John and Mary Sinclair learned of the gold discovery *before* Marshall met in secret with John Sutter.

If Mary indeed said this, then her memories, filtered through so many years, seem to have telescoped other incidents into one event and confused another trail—which *did* traverse the Rancho del Paso headed north toward the Feather and Yuba Rivers—with the route between Sutter's Fort and Coloma. The Coloma route ran well south of the American River almost the entire distance. The rain-lashed, mud-splattered path Marshall took on January 28, 1848 to meet with Captain Sutter did not take him through the Sinclair's property. Moreover, Marshall had no reason to cross a rain-swollen river merely to "drop in" on the Sinclairs when he was in such haste to reach Sutter, his partner in the sawmill project. The couple had known James Marshall since the latter's arrival at Sutter's Fort in 1845, and John did go to Marshall's mountain mill site camp in early April 1848. Undoubtedly, he returned with some shining samples to show Mary before he headed back out to establish his own claim elsewhere, thus creating Mary's misremembrance. The same article quotes Mary as saying that she was the first white woman married in Mexican California, and the mother of the first white child born there, both untrue, yet apparently unchallenged in the fervor that characterized this festive occasion.[105]

Also wholeheartedly accepted by her fellow New England Associated California Pioneers members was Mary's assertion that she and John had been "bosom friends" of John Sutter, dead since 1880, but firmly enshrined in the hearts of hundreds of California pioneers as their literal savior from destitution. True, the respective Sutter and Sinclair ranches were geographically close and, isolated as they both were from the larger population centers along the coast, indeed depended on one another. Sutter and Sinclair engaged in cattle trading and stock breeding between themselves, and Sinclair's prized Merino ram was meant to eventually produce a finer quality of wool in both of their flocks. Shared conditions and experiences united them against the daily and seasonal challenges a backwater environment imposed. It is our loss that their ordinary personal interchanges lay outside the margins of historical records.

Certain other factors, though, suggest that Mary's claim of a close friendship with Sutter requires further examination. Certainly, John Sutter would have displayed his elegant manners and considerable personal charm to Mary. One can imagine laughter at the dinner table and even kindly, indulgent advice from a cultured gentleman to a lady who was, after all, young enough to be his daughter. But Sutter, in his later interviews long after John Sinclair's death, spoke of him almost dismissively. For instance, Sutter never forgot nor forgave what he characterized as Sinclair's "cowardly desertion" during the Micheltorena campaign. Perhaps the root of Sutter's feelings was the fact that John Sinclair emerged atop the local economic heap, whereas Sutter himself suffered financial ruin. Be that as it may, Sutter's older-years attitude indicates that the on-going relationship with an early-days associate was far more complex than Mary's interpretation of a long-ago life let on. The *New Helvetia Diary* records the presence of John Sinclair at Sutter's Fort more than forty times between September 1845 and May 1848. Mary is never mentioned by name, although the *Diary* does identify and record the comings and goings of other women. It would seem that, unless Mary Sinclair was included in the *Diary*'s several "Many of the neighbors were here today" entries, she met and spoke with Captain Sutter in her own home, on infrequent occasions.

In the end, then, Mary too is a ghost-like wisp in John Augustus Sutter's historic saga. If later on she glorified or exaggerated her acquaintance with him she wasn't alone. So did hundreds of gold-rushers who chanced to meet him in person, in the midst of the greatest adventure of their lives. That Mary Sinclair chose to spend her time at home attending to her own responsibilities only underscores her important, though inglorious and often under-appreciated, role as a hard-working pioneer wife in pre-statehood California.

Mary told her descendants that she had been an English child of ten when she marched in the procession on the day of Queen Victoria's coronation.[106] At fifteen she sailed across the Atlantic Ocean to the United States and at sixteen, traveled across a continent in a covered wagon. She escaped a cruel father with the help of frontiering Americans, and became the mistress of an enormous Sacramento Valley ranch before she was twenty. The pioneers she and John knew, those whose names and deeds resonate throughout northern California history, comprise an impressive list: John Sutter, Joseph Ballinger Chiles, William Baldridge, Pierson B. Reading, Joseph R. Walker, George Yount and his daughters, Thomas Oliver Larkin, Samuel Hensley, Sarah Montgomery Wallis, the Martin Murphy and Thomas Rhoads families, Jared Sheldon and William Daylor, James and Margret Reed, Peter Burnett, Samuel Kyburz, Julius and Elizabeth Martin, Stockton founder Charles Weber, Chico founder John Bidwell, James Marshall, Sam Brannan and a host of others. Mary Sinclair outlived most of them—lived to see those new-fangled auto-mobiles careen about Boston streets in place of horse-drawn buggies.

Surrounded by her children and grandchildren, Mary Sinclair Davis died in her home of many years at 18 St. James Place, Roxbury (currently a suburb of Boston) on July 2, 1909, of "prostration of the heart caused by enfeeblement from age." She was 82. Funeral services were held in her residence on July 6. She is buried in Lexington, Massachusetts.[107]

The large Davis family headstone in Munroe Cemetery lists those who are interred beneath it. The names of Sidney Glass Davis and Mary Sinclair Davis (albeit with an incorrect birth year) are followed by two of their six children.

At the bottom, below a carved line, is the name John Sinclair, 1809-1849. He is not buried there. That his name is etched on another family's grave marker is almost positive evidence that he was indeed buried at sea, and this is his only memoriam.

Davis Family headstone Munroe Cemetery, Lexington, Massachusetts.
Photograph by Lori Hall, used with permission.

# APPENDIX I

John Sinclair's letter to Alcalde Washington Allon Bartlett in San Francisco
*Note: This letter, based on William Eddy's sickbed-written report, was penned before Sinclair interviewed the survivors himself. The seven indented lines beginning with "and each sat sullenly apart" are excerpts from Lord Byron's 1816 poem "Darkness," a testimony to Sinclair's undocumented yet clearly classical education. The letter itself, as published in the Ohio Observer October 16, 1847, is courtesy of Kristin Johnson.*

Rancho del Paso, January 29, 1847

The following narrative of facts, so far as I have learned them, may be depended on; a full and perfect narrative I am not able to give you, not having, as yet, seen any of the unfortunate sufferers. It appears that about the 18th of December, nine men, five women, and two Indians, in the employ of Capt. Sutter, left what is called Reid's [sic] party of emigrants, who have been detained in the mountains by the snow, with intention of reaching this settlement, driven to this course by the certain death which awaited them in [the] mountains. They started, in a manner of speaking, without provisions (one of the men having only two pounds of beef.) And, as you will understand, on foot, the snow being then where they were ten feet deep. A few days afterwards two of the men became so weak that they concluded to turn back. These two, it is supposed, perished. The rest endeavored to struggle on a while, every hour beholding them getting weaker, until they were obligated to throw away the blankets which they carried to shield them from the piercing cold, which in those regions is intense. At [what] time they go entirely out of provisions I am unable to say, but in the midst of their sufferings a snow storm came on, which lasted three days and three nights; and during the whole time they were without fire, and as far as I have understood without food. During these three dreadful days and nights they sat huddled together in the snow, their heads resting upon their knees, exposed to the pitiless storm! Great God! Who can imagine the sufferings of these helpless, houseless beings, at that time, without food and without fire?—no prospects before them but death, and that death the most horrible which can fall to the lot of man!

After the storm ceased they succeeded in getting fire, and again endeavored to pursue their pathless course through the newly fallen snow. Whether any of the party died previous to this I cannot say; but if not, death was there hovering fearfully over them. Again they camped—

"—and each sat sullenly apart,
Gorging himself in gloom: no love was left;
All earth was but one thought, and that was death.
Immediate and inglorious: and the pant
Of famine fed upon all entrails. Men
Died, and their bones were tombless as their flesh—
The meager by the meager were devoured."

Yes, stern necessity, and the love of life which even sufferings the most intense cannot vanquish, compelled them to devour their dead.

Let me close this tale of horror. Suffice it to say that seven out of the sixteen reached the settlement forty miles above me—five women two men. The rest died at different times, and six of them became food for the living. The two Indians who had been sent there early in the season by Capt. Sutter with provisions, were the last that died, and they likewise were eaten, with the exception of their heads. Those who escaped arrived with hardly sufficient clothing to cover their nakedness, their clothes being nearly burnt from their backs by keeping as close to their fires, and most of them having their feet badly frozen. They were one month on the road the distance being only about one hundred and ten miles. They report [those] remaining [in the] mountains still alive, by eating the bullock hides, and being on short allowances, may have provisions up to the middle of next month.

Mr. Kern, Capt. Sutter, Mr. McKinstry, and myself, are doing all we can to raise men to go to the assistance of those in the mountains, and have pledged ourselves to pay each man three dollars per day from the time they start until they return, provided the emigrants themselves should not be able to pay.—We likewise hold ourselves responsible for the provisions, at the same time we feel confident that our government will be willing to pay all expenses incurred in such a case as this, and we know that there is not one of our fellow citizens but is willing to aid and assist us in saving the lives of those helpless women and children.

By the 2nd of February, I think, about fourteen men will be able to start, which will be nearly every able-bodied man in the vicinity, and I would urge the propriety of calling a meeting of the inhabitants of Yerba Buena, and from among them endeavor to raise about twenty able-bodied men to form a second party [to] go to their assistance, as the men who are going from here will not be able to go back.—Capt. Hull will likewise, undoubtedly, exert all his influence and authority in furthering such an undertaking.

You will excuse this hasty sketch of their sufferings, as I have not time to be more explicit. I leave here tomorrow on foot for the starting point, distant forty miles, to bring on and complete everything for the expedition.

You will oblige me by making this communication as public as possible; as I wish everyone to know the situation of these unfortunate people, in order that it may stir them to exertion in their behalf.

I remain yours, respectfully,

John Sinclair

# APPENDIX II

## THE EYRE FAMILY
### (Sometimes misspelled Eyres, or Ayres, in various sources)

### Miles Eyre
b. March 24, 1799, Yorkshire, England

m. Eliza Turner October 2, 1825, at Parish Church of Newark, England

d. September 26, 1843, Oregon Territory

### Eliza Turner Eyre
b. November 25, 1805, Newark, England

m1. Miles Eyre, 1825, in England

m2. John Campbell, c. 1847 in Oregon; divorced 1848

m3. John Hobson November 10, 1853, in Oregon

d. December 14, 1893, in Portland, Oregon

### Mary Miles Eyre
b. March 29, 1827, Chard Parish, Somerset, England

m1. John Sinclair, 1844, Napa Valley, California

m2. Sidney Glass Davis, November 25, 1852, Lexington, Massachusetts

d. July 2, 1909, in Roxbury, Massachusetts

### Thomas Turner Eyre
b. April 10, 1829, Chard Parish, Somerset, England

m. Abbie Coffin, 1858, in Oregon; married Mary E. after 1870, year unknown

d. unknown. Living in Florida in 1900, orange grower, divorced

### Eliza Eyre
b. May 5, 1831, Nottingham, England

m1. William K. Beale c. 1846, in Oregon

m2. John E. Shepherd, in Oregon, year unknown

d. July 10, 1909, in Portland, Oregon

## Amelia Eyre

b. October 15, 1835, Linton, England

m. Charles F. Ray, in Oregon, year unknown

d. March, 1909, in Oregon

# END NOTES

1. Hammond, *The Larkin Papers* 4:332. Report from Thomas O. Larkin to Secretary of State James Buchanan dated June 1846, "Description of California and the personal character of [its] principal men."

2. Passenger & Immigration Lists New Orleans, 1820-1850, posted on the Metzer-Engquist Family Home Page (descendants of Eliza Turner Eyre). See Appendix II for Eyre family statistics, from the Eyre Family File, Oregon Historical Society.

3. Signed St. Louis Circuit Court document dated March 24, 1842. Copy of original obtained from Missouri State Archives, County of St. Louis Naturalization Record Vol. T, Page 32, Reel C2 5-809; the *St. Louis Directory for the Year 1842*, pg. 42; *Sacramento Daily Union* May 5, 1876, "City Intelligence" column, interview with Mrs. Eliza Eyre Shepherd.

4. Campbell vs. Eyre divorce proceedings filed/granted in Oregon, from the Metzer- Engquist Family Home Page; *Oregonian* July 11, 1909, Susannah and John Campbell listed as surviving siblings in the obituary of Eliza Eyre Shepherd.

5. Drury, *Marcus and Narcissa Whitman and the Opening of Old Oregon,* Chapters 18 and 19.

6. Drury, *Whitman and the Opening of Old Oregon.* "The Oregon Emigration Party," an anonymous letter published in the *Loraine Republican,* August 1843, whose author was with Dr. Whitman on June 3, 1843. Also see Coffman, *Blazing a Wagon Trail to Oregon; "Journal of John Boardman,"* entry dated June 3; and Burnett, *Recollections of an Old Pioneer.* The location was in present-day Topeka, Kansas.

7. Coffman, *Blazing a Wagon Trail to Oregon*. Eyre family in company with Daniel Waldo and the Applegate brothers, see interview with Mrs. Eliza Eyre Shepherd, *Sacramento Daily Union* May 5, 1876.

8. The Chiles Party was still at Elm Grove (30 miles west of Westport) on May 31, as noted in John Frémont's report of his explorations; quoted in Hubert Bancroft, *History of California*, 5:392. See also Lewis, *Pioneers of California*; Stewart, *The California Trail;* and *History of Napa and Lake Counties*.

9. Arrival Fort Laramie, "Journal of John Boardman." Mary's tale is found in *History of the Town of Lexington*.

10. "Journal of John Boardman." Also Gilbert, *Westering Man* pp. 174-197 and Coffman, *Blazing a Wagon Trail to Oregon*, p. 89.

11. The Eyre Family File, Oregon Historical Society, gives Miles's death as September 26, 1843. For "Prairie Flower," see biographical sketch of William Baldridge, *History of Napa and Lake Counties*. Eyre family at Waiilatpu winter of 1843-44 documented in Clifford Drury, *Marcus and Narcissa Whitman*.

12. *History of Napa and Lake Counties*; Gilbert, *Westering Man* pp. 174-197. Quote, "Journal of John Boardman."

13. Bancroft, *History of California* 4:393. Helen Giffen, *Trail-Blazing Pioneer* p. 40, says there were eleven men.

14. Gilbert, *Westering Man;* Stewart, *The California Trail; History of Santa Clara County;* Bancroft, *History of California*. Bancroft says that Joseph R. Walker and Lt. Edward Kern knowingly "passed by" these implements in 1845, but also notes Baldridge's claim that they were first found by miners in 1863. Milton Little settled at Monterey as a trader in 1844.

15. Date and time December 3, 1843 at 11:00 a.m. from the biographical sketch of William Baldridge, *History of Napa and Lake Counties,* pp. 387-394. Also see "The California Immigrant Company of 1843" in San Francisco *Daily Evening Bulletin* July 20, 1860, and biographical sketch of Julius Martin in *History of Santa Clara County,* pp. 616-618.

16. Baldridge bio sketch in *History of Napa and Lake Counties.* From Bancroft 4:393: Walker, Anderson, Dawson and Cowie applied for passports in Monterey in February 1844. Evidently, Lewis Anderson accompanied Joseph Walker east with the herd in April. Thomas Cowie was killed during the Bear Flag Revolt.

17. Biographical sketch of Julius Martin in *History of Santa Clara County,* pp. 616-618.

18. Chiles' horseback riders arrival at Sutter's Fort in Gilbert, *Westering Man,* p. 195, and Munro-Fraser, *History of Contra Costa County,* p. 513. Baldridge and James "Old Wheat" Atkinson were aided by James Hudspeth and Alexander Copeland, who were working in the surrounding redwoods. In June of that year both Hudspeth and Copeland moved to Sutter's Fort. The Williams brothers remained for a time at the fort, where James Williams worked as a blacksmith and John Williams as a tanner. Afterward all four brothers settled in the Santa Cruz area. Also see Baldridge bio sketch as previously cited.

19. Sinclair prospering: Bancroft, 5:721. The Hawaiian Archives, a collection of data dating no farther back than 1841, has no record of this marriage, or a daughter, who would have been born in 1839. Her whereabouts in 1844 are unknown.

20. *The Correspondence and Journals of Nathaniel J. Wyeth.*

21. *Ibid.* Quote, p. 178.

22. John Ball, "Across the Continent Seventy Years Ago." This *Dryad*, purchased by the HBC in 1829 and used for its Pacific Northwest trade, was not the same-named ship used in the African slave trade in the early 1830s. John Ball's journal makes it clear that most of Sinclair's time in Oregon was spent as an independent farmer and not as a Hudson's Bay Company employee.

23. National Maritime Digital Library, *Helvetius.*

24. St. Clair, "Hawaii's HBC History," re George Pelly. Also William J. Breault, *John A. Sutter in Hawaii.* Based on Sinclair's statements to Billy Baldridge about his marriage to a Hawaiian woman and their daughter, it appears that he was living in Hawaii the entire time since the wreck of the *Helvetius* at Oahu in 1834.

25. Greer, "Honolulu in 1838," referencing *Sandwich Island Gazette* for August 11 and 25, 1838. Neither this source nor the Hawaiian State Archives contains definitive documentation that indeed Sinclair "stood in" during Macintosh's vacation.

26. William J. Breault, *John A. Sutter in Hawaii.*

27. Quote in Erwin Gudde, *Sutter's Own Story,* p. 92. Sinclair at Monterey in December 1839, at Sutter's 1840, Bancroft 5:721. Fort description Hurtado, *John Sutter.*

28. Breault, pp. 61-62, quoting excerpts from the Sutter Collection 1840-1861: Ms. 62-4747; Papers: 1840-1879. What Sutter meant by "castor furs" was beaver skins known in the fur trade as *castor gras*: beaver that had been worn for a year or more until the long, outer hairs fell off leaving only the inner coat—the best fur for felting, used in the manufacture of top hats.

29. Allgeier/Keyser arrival, *Diary of Johann August Sutter,* and William Wiggins' statement. Sinclair letter to Davis in Zollinger, p. 117. Sinclair becomes Mexican citizen: Bancroft 5:721. Yerba Buena was San Francisco's original name.

30. Kibbey, *Sacramento Directory 1851*, "Sacramento History" p. 43. Sinclair takes possession in early 1842, Bancroft 4:566 and 5:721. Also see Oliver, *Rancho del Paso*, Appendix 1 and 2.

31. Phelps, *Alta California 1840-1842, the Journal and Observations of William Dane Phelps*.

32. *Ibid.*

33. Yates, *A Sailor's Sketch*, p. 16.

34. Sandels, *A Sojourn in California by the King's Orphan*, pp. 55-61.

35. Oliver, *Rancho del Paso*, pp. 2–8.

36. Nunis, *Journal of a Sea Captain's Wife*, p.157; description of Mary Eyre in Bryant, *What I Saw in California*, p. 246.

37. Higuera's ranch in Wallace, *History of Napa County*. Year and place of Sinclair marriage from *History of the Town of Lexington*, p. 165; *Sacramento Daily Union* May 4 and 5, 1876, interviews with Mary Sinclair's sister Mrs. Eliza Eyre Beale Shepherd "The First White Woman on the American," and "City Intelligence." Baldridge bio sketch as previously cited.

38. David J. Langum, "Expatriate Domestic Relations Law in Mexican California."

39. Alan Rosenus, *General Vallejo and the Advent of the Americans*.

40. Frémont, *The Exploring Expedition to the Rocky Mountains, Oregon and California*, pp. 352-354.

41. *Sacramento Union* April 22, 1892 "New England Pioneers."

42. Steve Beck, Sutter's Fort SHP; Lewis, *Pioneers of California* pp. 505-509. "White" in 19th century California meant non-Indian.

43. James Rose, "Saga of the Stephens-Townsend-Murphy Party of 1844" Part 2.

44. Gudde, *Sutter's Own Story* pp. 107-123; Dillon, *Captain John Sutter,* p. 181; and J. A. Sutter's correspondence to P. B. Reading April 24, 1844 to May 11, 1846.

45. *New Helvetia Diary*; Stewart, *The California Trail.* Texas ratified annexation in July, and became a state in December 1845.

46. *Larkin Papers,* Vol. III. Letter to Thomas Larkin from John Sutter dated July 22, 1845; Dillon, pp. 203-204.

47. *New Helvetia Diary* pp. 16, 17, 20, 23, 25, 31, 40.

48. *Diary of Johann August Sutter.* Dillon, pp. 244-249. Frémont's Legislative Council appointments from the *California Star* February 6, 1847. Also see DeVoto, *Year of Decision* pp. 261, 472.

49. Bancroft, 5:721 and 5:462-468; *Sutter and a Wider West*, p. 18.

50. Bryant, pp. 245-246.

51. *Larkin Papers*, Vol. II p.184.

52. Wilber, *A Pioneer at Sutter's Fort.* Erwin and Elisabeth Gudde's translation of Lienhard's journals say the fruit was wild grapes.

53. Ricketts, *Historic Cosumnes and the Slough House Pioneer Cemetery.*

54. Stewart, *Ordeal by Hunger* pp. 142 -153.

55. A second letter by John Sinclair dated February 1847 is printed in Bryant, pp. 251-255.

56. Stewart, p. 177; McGlashan, p. 73; Morgan, *Overland in 1846,* "Diaries of the Donner Relief" pp. 323-336.

57. Donner Party files, Sutter's Fort Archives. *New Helvetia Diary*, p. 48.

58. Stewart, *Ordeal by Hunger* p. 206, pp. 365-67.

59. Eliza Donner Houghton, *The Expedition of the Donner Party and its Tragic Fate,* Ch.15.

60. Ricketts, *Historic Cosumnes and the Slough House Pioneer Cemetery.*

61. Stewart, p. 287; *New Helvetia Diary* May 22, 1847.

62. Sutter's Fort Archives; *New Helvetia Diary.* Yates, A *Sailor's Sketch* p. 4.

63. Letter from John Sinclair to James Frazier Reed June 23, 1847, Sutter's Fort Archives. The phrase "rounds apace" is from Shakespeare's *Winter's Tale* Act 2, Scene 1, "the queen your mother rounds apace; we shall present our services to a fine new prince one of these days." Sinclair's use of "lusty" is from Shakespeare's *Henry V,* defined in the play's context as vigorous, strong, robust, and eager.

64. *Sutter's Own Story* p. 179; *New Helvetia Diary* p. 53; Dillon, *Captain John Sutter,* p. 263-265.

65. Wilber, *A Pioneer at Sutter's Fort*, p. 28. Oliver, pp. 10-11. *New Helvetia Diary* pp. 47, 88, 90, 100.

66. Introduction to John Yates, *A Sailor's Sketch;* also Steed, *The Donner Party Rescue Site — Johnson's Ranch on Bear River.*

67. *Sutter's Own Story* p. 182; *New Helvetia Diary*

68. *New Helvetia Diary* pp. 46, 84-85, 101, 106, 112.

69. Wilber, *A Pioneer at Sutter's Fort* pp. 91-92; *New Helvetia Diary* pp. 114-115; Bancroft, *Pioneer Register.*

70. *New Helvetia Diary* pp. 116-117, Dupas vs. Cox; p. 122, Dupas vs. Daylor.

71. *New Helvetia Diary* pp. 126-127, Kadel vs. Salinas March 30, 1848; also see p. 72, Salinas takes a horse from Hockmulla "on which he had no claim."

72. *New Helvetia Diary* pp. 120-130; Lavender, p. 156.

73. Mason, Col. Richard Barnes, "Report on the California Gold Discoveries." Kyle, *Historic Spots in California* p. 274.

74. R. C. Wyllie's letter to John Sinclair dated October 10, 1848, courtesy of the Hawaii State Archives.

75. Wilber, *Adventures of Heinrich Lienhard*, p. 120; *New Helvetia Diary* p. 130.

76. "Grimshaw's Narrative," p. 24. Colton, "First Reports of 1848 Gold Discovery Reach Monterey."

77. Mason, Col. R., "Report on the California Gold Discoveries." Sherman, *Recollections of California 1846-1861.* Also see Gudde, *Sutter's Own Story*, p. 213-215.

78. *Sacramento Daily Union* March 16, 1890, reprinted from the Boston *Herald.* This story, related so many years after the event, has some inconsistencies. Either Mary—or the reporter—mistakenly said that the year was 1847,

and the article suggests that the occasion was a ball at Sutter's Fort arranged by Sherman and his military associates. However, Lt. Wm. Sherman was at Sutter's Fort for the first time during the July 4th celebration in 1848, and took no part in planning the activities. Also see Sherman, *Recollections of California 1846-1861.*

79. Wilber, pg. 167.

80. *Larkin Papers* Vol. VII, pp. 338-339. Letter to Thomas Larkin from Moses Schallenberger dated August 16, 1848. *Larkin Papers* Vol. VII, p. 332, letter to Thomas Larkin from Charles Sterling; also pp. 338-339 and 341-342. Cattle count in Davis, *Seventy-five Years in California*, p. 158.

81. United States Senate 1850, *Message from the President of the United States*, pp. 462, 463, 465, letters from Col. Richard B. Mason to Alcalde John Sinclair.

82. Either Heinrich Lienhard, or his translator Ms. Wilber, confuses the names of the two Bates brothers. Henry Bates was the doctor; Franklin the alcalde. Dr. Henry Bates opened a hospital at Coloma in May 1849, *Placer Times* May 12, 1849. Re Franklin Bates, see *Sacramento Union* May 14-15, 1855, "Pioneer Criminal Trial in Sacramento."

83. *Californian* "Marine Intelligence" September 30 and October 14, 1848; *Oregon Free Press* November 11, October 14, September 9, 1848.

84. *Sacramento Daily Union* May 5, 1876. Commentary regarding the founding of Beale's Bar, a mining camp located above the point where the North and South Forks of the American River meet, is from Eliza Eyre Beale Shepherd's interview in this article.

85. *Sacramento Daily Union* October 6, 1855, "Fatal Accident." [at Beale's Bar]

86. John A. Sutter Jr., *The Sutter Family.*

87. *Sacramento Daily Union* May 5, 1876. Kibbey, *Sacramento City Directory for the Year 1851* (bio sketches) p. 121, 126.

88. *California Star & Californian* December 16, 1848, "Murder at Sutter's Fort." December 23, 1848, "Acquittal of C.E. Pickett." Also see "Grimshaw's Narrative," p. 15; *Sacramento Daily Union* May 14-15, 1855.

89. Quote and other details of January meetings in Sacramento from *Weekly Alta California* January 18, 25, 1849. Sacramento's first newspaper *The Placer Times* didn't begin publishing until April 1849, and coastal newspapers didn't report the evolving status of Sacramento District delegates in this initial movement for a provisional government convention, which was indeed reset for May 1st, and then delayed again. Nothing further of note occurred until General Bennett Riley's proclamation dated June 3, 1849, mandated a constitutional convention to convene at Monterey in September.

90. *California Star & Californian* November 18, 1848; *Alta California* January 18, April 12, 1849; *Placer Times* October 27, November 10, 1849. Also see Mary's bio in *History of the Town of Lexington*.

91. Oliver, *Rancho del Paso*.

92. Chiles' itinerary in Lewis, *Pioneers of California* and Stewart, *California Trail*. Hiram Grimes sold the Rancho del Paso to Samuel Norris, a merchant with outlets at both San Francisco and Sutter's Fort, on August 8, 1849, for $8,000. By the early 1850s the rancho's original name was forgotten, retaining the identity "Norris Ranch" for several years even after Norris lost the property to his attorneys James B. Haggin and Lloyd Tevis in 1862. Oliver, *Rancho del Paso*.

93. *Weekly Alta California* April 5 – May 10, 1849, "Marine Journal;" details, ship *California* to/from San Francisco and Panama, see Captain Forbes' two journals in Pomfret, *California Gold Rush Voyages*; and "Diary of Mrs. Jane McDougal" in *Ho! For California*.

94. *Daily Picayune* (New Orleans) June 12, 1849; *The Sun* (Baltimore) June 19, 1849; *Daily Union* (Washington, D.C.) June 27, 1849; *Alta California* August 30, 1849; *History of Lexington*, p. 165.

95. New York Public Library archives: Official Probate Records of the County of New York 1849, records Sinclair's Last Will and Testament, witness statements, and other probate-related documents.

96. The levy breach occurred on May 3, 1849 and was not plugged until June 20. Richard Campanella, "Sauvé's Crevasse." Beth Davis at Louisiana Secretary of State Archives in Baton Rouge, states that before 1952, when funeral homes took over the task of filing death certificates, it is not unusual for there to be *no* certificate on file. Contrary to popular belief, burial belowground has always been practiced in the region for cultural or economic reasons having nothing to do with water tables.

97. *The Spectator* (New York) June 28, 1849, "The Owners of the Gold."

98. *Weekly Alta California* August 30, 1849.

99. Phelps, *Fore and Aft*, p. 320.

100. *History of the Town of Lexington* pp. 178-179; Federal Census, 1850. Also see Introduction pg. 31-32 of Phelps' journal, for reference to Thomas & Rachel Larkin.

101. Hammond, *The Larkin Papers* Vol. VII, pp.402-403.

102. *History of the Town of Lexington*, p. 165; Massachusetts Deaths, 1841-1915 database.

103. *Sacramento Daily Union* March 16, 1890, quoting the Boston *Herald*.

104. *Sacramento Daily Union* November 18, 1890, "In Memory of Old," and April 22, 1892, "New England Pioneers." *Sacramento Daily Union* July 10, 1893, "Pioneers of Forty-Nine."

105. *San Francisco Call* January 25, 1898, a Special Dispatch to *The Call* from Boston. This story was repeated in the *Kansas City Journal*, with its own flourishes, on February 6, 1898. Surely this misinformation comes from the newspaperman's fanciful imagination, not Mary, who should not have forgotten her predecessors to such claims; in particular Rachel (Mrs. Thomas) Larkin, an American whose several children were born in Monterey beginning in 1833. Mary also knew that Englishwoman Eliza Gregson gave birth to a daughter at Sutter's Fort in 1846, the year before her own daughter was born. But then, many early-days pioneer women succumbed to this type of braggadocio in their later lives. One example (of several) of a marriage pre-dating Mary's nuptials is that of Lizzie Sumner and George Davis, migrants from Oregon who wed at Sutter's Fort in 1843.

106. *History of the Town of Lexington* p. 165.

107. *Boston Herald* July 6, 1909; Death Certificate #5855, Boston, filed July 6, 1909.

# BIBLIOGRAPHY

**Newspapers**
*Alta California*
*Boston Daily Bee*
*Boston Herald*
*Boston Traveler*
*Brooklyn Daily Eagle*
*California Star*
*California Star & Californian*
*Californian*
*Daily Atlas* (Boston)
*Daily Picayune* (New Orleans)
*Daily Evening Bulletin* (San Francisco)
*Daily Union* (Washington, D. C.)
*Kansas City Journal*
*Massachusetts Spy* (Worcester)
*New Orleans Bee*
*Oregonian* (Portland)
*Oregon Free Press* (Oregon City)
*Placer Times* (Sacramento)
*Sacramento Daily Union,* 1855-1896
*Sandwich Islands Gazette* (Hawaii)
*The Spectator* (New York)
*The Sun* (Baltimore, MD)


**Books, Periodicals, Manuscripts**
Author unknown. "The Oregon Emigration Party." A letter written by an emigrant on the Kansas River dated June 3, 1843 and printed in the *Loraine Republican*, Lorain, Ohio, edition 9, August 1843. Originally published in the *Iowa Gazette* July 8, 1843.

Ball, John. "Across the Continent Seventy Years Ago." Excerpts published in *The Quarterly of the Oregon Historical Society Vol. III* March, 1902.

Bancroft, Hubert H. *History of California Vol. IV, 1840-1845*. San Francisco, CA: The History Company, 1886.

Beck, Steve, History Program Lead at Sutter's Fort State Historic Park, Sacramento. Personal discussions.

Beck, Steve. "1844 Stephens/Murphy/Townsend Party, A Brief Narrative," and "Notes on Agriculture and the Grist Mill at New Helvetia." Manuscripts courtesy Sutter's Fort State Historic Park.

Boardman, John. Published as "The Journal of John Boardman, An Overland Journey from Kansas to Oregon in 1843." J. Cecil Alter, editor, *Utah Historical Quarterly* Vol. 2, No. 4. Salt Lake City, October 1929.

Burnett, Peter H. *Recollections and Opinions of an Old Pioneer*. New York: D. Appleton and Company, 1880.

Breault, William J. *John A Sutter in Hawaii and California 1838-1839*. Rancho Cordova, California: Landmark Enterprises, 1998.

Bryant, Edwin. *What I Saw in California*. Lincoln, Nebraska: University of Nebraska Press, 1985.

California Supreme Court. *Reports of Cases Determined in the Supreme Court of the State of California*. 1906. Original from the University of California digitized 7/30/2009.

Campanella, Richard. "Sauvé's Crevasse." New Orleans *Times-Picayune* June 13, 2014.

Coffman, Lloyd W. *Blazing a Wagon Trail to Oregon, A Weekly Chronicle of the Great Migration of 1843*. Enterprise, Oregon: Echo Books, 1993.

Colton, Walter. "First Reports of 1848 Gold Discovery Reach Monterey." *California Territorial Quarterly* #84, 2010 Winter Issue.

Davis, William Heath. *Seventy-five Years in California*. Washington, D.C.: Westphalia Press edition, 2015.

DeVoto, Bernard. *The Year of Decision: 1846*. New York: Truman Tally Books, Year 2000 edition.

DeVoto, Bernard. *Across the Wide Missouri*. New York: Mariner Books edition, Houghton Mifflin Company, 1998.

Dillon, Richard. *Captain John Sutter: Sacramento Valley's Sainted Sinner*. Santa Cruz, California: Western Tanager, 1981.

Drury, Clifford M. *Marcus and Narcissa Whitman and the Opening of Old Oregon*. Seattle, Washington: Northwest Interpretive Association, © 1986; New Edition 2005.

Eells, Rev. Myron. *Marcus Whitman M.D. Proofs of his Work in Saving Oregon to the United States, and in Promoting the Immigration of 1843*. Portland, Oregon: George H. Himes and Jon Printing House, 1883.

Eyre Family File, courtesy of Oregon Historical Society, Portland, Oregon.

Fremont, Brevet Col. J. C. *The Exploring Expedition to the Rocky Mountains, Oregon and California to which is added a Description of the Physical Geography of California with Recent Notices of the Gold Region*. Buffalo: Geo. H. Derby and Co., Publishers 1851.

Giffen, Helen S. *Trail-Blazing Pioneer, Colonel Joseph Ballinger Chiles*. John Howell Books, 1969.

Gilbert, Bil. *Westering Man, The Life of Joseph Walker*. University of Oklahoma Press: 1983.

Gregson, James and Eliza. *The Gregson Memoirs, Containing Mrs. Eliza Gregson's "Memory" and the Statement of James Gregson*. San Francisco: Reprinted from California Historical Society Quarterly Vol. XIX No. 2, June 1940.

Greer, Richard A. "Honolulu in 1838." Honolulu: *Hawaiian Journal of History*, Vol. II, 1977. Retrieved from evols.library.manoa.hawaii.edu/handle/10524/176.

Gudde, Erwin G. *Sutter's Own Story, The Life of General John Augustus Sutter and the History of New Helvetia in the Sacramento Valley*. New York: G. P. Putnam's Sons, 1936.

Hawaii State Archives, Honolulu.

Hammond, George P., editor. *The Larkin Papers — Personal, Business, and Official Correspondence of Thomas Oliver Larkin, Merchant and United States Consul in California*. Vols. II-VIII. Berkeley: University of California Press, 1952-1962.

*History of Napa and Lake Counties, California*. San Francisco: Slocum, Bowen & Co., Publishers, 1881.

*History of Santa Clara County, California*. San Francisco: Alley, Bowen & Co., Publishers, 1881.

Holliday, J.S. *The World Rushed In*. University of Oklahoma Press, 2002.

Holmes, Kenneth L., editor. *Covered Wagon Women: Diaries & Letters from the Western Trails, 1840-1849*. Lincoln: University of Nebraska Press Bison Books edition, 1995.

Houghton, Eliza P. Donner. *Expedition of the Donner Party and its Tragic Fate*. E-book version at scienceviews.com/historical/donnerparty.html. Originally published in book form 1911.

Hudson, Charles. *History of the Town of Lexington Middlesex County Massachusetts*. Lexington Historical Society Volume II, Genealogies. Boston: Houghton Mifflin Company, 1913.

Jackson, Donald and Mary Lee Spence, eds. *The Expeditions of John Charles Fremont Vol. I, Travels from 1838-1844*. Urbana: University of Illinois Press, 1970.

Johnson, Kristin. "New Light on the Donner Party" at utahcrossroads.org.

Grimshaw, William Robinson. "Grimshaw's Narrative," written for the Bancroft Library in 1872. J.R.K Kantor, ed. Sacramento: Sacramento Book Collectors Club, 1964.

Kibbey, Mead, ed. *Facsimile Reproduction of the California State Library Copy of J. Horace Culver's Sacramento City Directory for the Year 1851, With a History of Sacramento to 1851, Biographical Sketches, and Informative Appendices.* Sacramento: California State Library Foundation, 2000.

Kibbey, Mead, ed. *Samuel Colville's Sacramento Directory for the Year 1853-54, Together with a History of Sacramento written by Dr. John F. Morse.* Sacramento: California State Library Foundation, 1997.

Kyle, Douglas E., ed. *Historic Spots in California*, Fifth Edition. Stanford, California: Stanford University Press, 2002.

Langum, David J. "Expatriate Domestic Relations Law in Mexican California." Pepperdine Law Review Volume 7, Issue 1, 1980.

Lavender, David. *California Land of New Beginnings.* University of Nebraska Press, 1972.

Lavender, David. *Westward Vision, The Story of the Oregon Trail.* University of Nebraska Press Bison Books Edition reprint 1985.

Lewis, Donovan. *Pioneers of California, True Stories of Early Settlers in the Golden State.* San Francisco: Scottwell Associates, 1993.

Morgan, Dale, ed. *Overland in 1846: Diaries and Letters of the California-Oregon Trail Vols. I and II.* University of Nebraska Press, 1993.

Mason, Colonel Richard. Official report on the California gold discoveries dated at Monterey August 17, 1848; printed December 8, 1848, in the *New York Daily Tribune.*

McGlashan, C. F. *History of the Donner Party, a Tragedy of the Sierra.* Lexington, Kentucky: Hardpress Inc., 2010.

Metzer/Engquist Family Homepage at familytreemaker.genealogy.com, downloaded 5/25/2014.

Miller, G. Andrew, historian. Unpublished research papers on Joseph Ballinger Chiles and Joseph Walker dated 11/25/2008.

Missouri State Archives, County of St. Louis. Naturalization Record Vol. T, Page 32, Reel C2 5-809, Miles Eyre.

Munro-Fraser, J. P. *History of Contra Costa County.* San Francisco: W. A. Slocum & Co., 1882.

Myres, Sandra L., ed. *Ho for California! Women's Overland Diaries from the Huntington Library*; "A Diary Kept by Mrs. Jane McDougal." San Marino, California: Huntington Library, 1980.

National Maritime Digital Library. American Offshore Whaling Voyages: A Database. Voyages of *Helvetius* (vessel #1569) stranded at Oahu, 1834.

New York Public Library. Official probate records of the County of New York 1849, courtesy of John R. Barlow, Curator for Business, History and Social Sciences.

Nunis, Doyce B. Jr., ed. *The Journal of a Sea Captain's Wife 1841-1845.* Spokane, Washington: The Arthur H. Clark Company, 2004.

Oliver, Raymond. *Rancho del Paso, A History of the Land Surrounding McClellan Air Force Base.* Sacramento: Office of History Sacramento Air Logistics Center McClellan Air Force Base, March 1983.

Phelps, William Dane. *Alta California 1840-1842, The Journal and Observations of William Dane Phelps, Master of the Ship "Alert."* Introduced and edited by Briton Cooper Busch. Glendale, CA: The Arthur H. Clark Company, 1983.

Phelps, William Dane. *Fore and Aft; or, Leaves From the Life of an Old Sailor.* Boston: Nichols & Hall, 1871.

Pomfret, John E., ed. *California Gold Rush Voyages, 1848-1849.* Westport, Connecticut: Greenwood Press, 1974.

Ricketts, Norma Baldwin. *Historic Cosumnes and the Slough House Pioneer Cemetery* (booklet). Salt Lake City, Utah: National Society Daughters of Utah Pioneers, 1978.

Rose, James J. "Saga of the Stephens-Townsend-Murphy Party of 1844," Parts 1 & 2. *Dogtown Territorial Quarterly* issues 18 & 19, 1994.

Rosenus, Alan. *General Vallejo and the Advent of the Americans.* Berkeley: Heyday Books, 1999.

Sandels, G. M. Waseurtz. *A Sojourn in California by the King's Orphan. The travels and sketches of G. M. Waseurtz af Sandels, a Swedish gentleman who visited California in 1842-1843.* Edited, with an introduction by Helen Putnam Van Sicklen. San Francisco: Grabhorn Press for the Book Club of California in arrangement with The Society of California Pioneers, 1945.

Sherman, General William T. *Recollections of California 1846-1861.* Oakland, CA: Biobooks, 1945.

Sinclair, John. Letters to James Frazer Reed dated June 23 and 25, 1847, and April 5, 1848; and other Sinclair-authored documents. Courtesy Sutter's Fort Historic State Park Archives.

Spenser, C., and Dr. Tucker, editors. *The Encyclopedia of the Mexican-American War: A Political, Social and Military History.* Santa Barbara, 2013.

St. Clair, William P. Jr. "Hawaii's HBC History," originally published in *The Beaver* magazine September 1941, reprinted in *Canada's History* magazine June-July 2014. canadashistory.ca/Magazine/Online-Extension/Articles/HBC-and-the-Northwest.

Steed, Jack. *The Donner Party Rescue Site — Johnson's Ranch on Bear River,* third edition. Sacramento, California 1993.

Stewart, George R. *The California Trail, An Epic With Many Heroes,* © 1962. University of Nebraska Press, 1983.

Sutter, J. A. Correspondence to P. B. Reading April 24, 1844 to May 11, 1846. Typescript and annotated index by Lucinda M. Woodward, 1981.

Sutter, J. A. "The Diary of Johann August Sutter," a.k.a. "The Statement of Johann August Sutter, 1856." Reprinted in *John Sutter and a Wider West,* Kenneth N. Owens, ed. University of Nebraska Press, 1994.

Sutter, John A. Jr. *The Sutter Family and the Origins of Gold Rush Sacramento*. Allan R. Ottley, ed. Norman, Oklahoma: Red River Books Edition, University of Oklahoma Press 2002.

Swackhamer, Barry. "California Pioneers James Williams (et al)." The Historical Marker Database HMdb.org. Marker is located in Santa Cruz.

Thornton, J. Quinn, edited by William R. Jones. *Camp of Death: The Donner Party Mountain Camp 1846-47.* Golden, CO: Outback Books, 1986.

United States Senate. *Message from the President of the United States Communicating Information Called for by a Resolution of the Senate of the 17th Instant, in Relation to California and New Mexico* — United States President (1849-1850: Z. Taylor) Washington, DC: January 1850.

Unruh, John D. Jr. *The Plains Across - The Overland Emigrants and the Trans-Mississippi West, 1840-60.* Chicago: University of Illinois Press, 1982.

Wallace, W. F. *History of Napa County.* Oakland: Enquirer Print, 1901.

Wiggins, William. "Reminiscences on California." Manuscript, dictated to Thomas Savage for the Bancroft Library, 1877.

Wilber, Marguerite Eyer, editor and translator. *A Pioneer at Sutter's Fort, 1846-1850; the Adventures of Heinrich Lienhard.* Los Angeles: The Califa Society, 1941.

Wyeth, Nathaniel Jarvis. *The Correspondence and Journals of Captain Nathaniel J. Wyeth, 1831-36.* F. G. Young, ed., Secretary Oregon Historical Society. Eugene, Oregon: University Press, 1899.

Yates, John. *A Sailor's Sketch of the Sacramento Valley in 1842.* Annotated by Ferol Egan. Berkeley, California: The Friends of the Bancroft Library, 1971.

Zollinger, J. Peter. *Sutter, The Man and His Empire.* Gloucester, Mass: Peter Smith, 1967.

# INDEX

# ABOUT THE AUTHOR

Cheryl Anne Stapp is the author of *Sacramento Chronicles — A Golden Past; The Stagecoach in Northern California: Rough Rides, Gold Camps & Daring Drivers;* and award-winning *Disaster & Triumph: Sacramento Women, Gold Rush Through the Civil War.* She lives in Sacramento, California, in bygone days an important Gold Rush town. Visit her website "California's Olden Golden Days" at http://cheryl-lannestapp.com.

Made in the USA
San Bernardino, CA
15 March 2017